FIGUREHEADS AND SHIP CARVING

MICHAEL STAMMERS

NAVAL INSTITUTE PRESS
ANNOPOLIS MARYLAND

Figureheads and Ship Carving

Copyright © 2005 by Michael Stammers

First published in Great Britain in 2005 by
Chatham Publishing,
Lionel Leventhal Limited,
Park House, 1 Russell Gardens, London NW11 9NN

Published and distributed in the United States of
Americaand Canada by the Naval institute Press, 291
Wood Road, Annapolis, Maryland 21402-5043

Library of Congress Control Number: 2005930018

ISBN 1-59114-274-1

Designed by Mousemat Design Limited

Printed and bound in Singapore

Title page: One of two stern carvings from the emigrant
clipper *Marco Polo*, 1851. (National Museums, Liverpool)

Acknowledgments

There are a number of people and institutions who
have contributed advice and pictures for this book
The photographs are credited with the captions.
May I thank (in no special order) Dawn Littler, John
Kearon and Tony Tibbles of the Merseyside
Maritime Museum, Captain George Hogg of the
National Maritime Museum Cornwall, Michael
McCaughan and Kenneth Anderson of Ulster Folk
and Transport Museum, Peter Ferguson and the vol-
unteers of the North Devon Maritime Museum,
Andy King of Bristol Industrial Museum, Klas
Helmerson and Sofi Aspelin of the Swedish National
Maritime Museums, Richard Doughty of the Cutty
Sark Trust, Richard Holdsworth and Alison Marsh of
the Chatham Historic Dockyard, Stephen Riley of
the National Maritime Museum, Adrian Osler,
formerly of Tyne and Wear Museums, Valerie
Fenwick of the Nautical Archaeology Society,
Campbell McCutcheon of Tempus Publishing,
Helen Doe, a descendant of Jane Slade, Mark Myers,
marine artist, Tony Lewery, author and painter of
canal boats, Arthur Credland of Hull Maritime
Museum, Aneesa Thomas of Roy, Utah for sharing
her research on David Hughes, and my wife for her
patience.

Contents

The decorative scheme of the frigate *Indefatigable* was typical of the last sailing warships with a figure-head painted white, a broad white band and simple carved mouldings around her round stern. (National Museums Liverpool)

Inset: Her figurehead as restored by her Old Boys Association in the late 1990s. (National Museums Liverpool)

CHAPTER

The Figurehead

A figurehead is 'an ornamental figure erected on the continuation of a ship's stem, as being expressive of her name, and emblematical of war, navigation, commerce, etc'. That was William Falconer's definition in his *Universal Dictionary of the Marine or, a copious explanation of the Technical Terms and Phrases employed in the construction, equipment, furniture, machinery, movements and military operations of a Ship,* published in 1780. They don't write titles like that any more, but Falconer's definition holds good today. The figurehead was one of the decorative elements of many sailing ships and a few steam and motor ships. It had no function except in the intangible sense of representing or symbolising the name of the ship and from that, if you want to be mystical, the 'soul' of the ship, and as a pleasing piece of decoration. Ships

The topsail schooner *Lochranza Castle* built at Wick in 1876.

A wool merchant's carved sign at the Strangers' Hall Museum, Norwich. (Norfolk Museums Service)

have always been the largest moveable objects made by Man from Noah's Ark onwards. As a result, they have had a special importance. They were seen as female and made maiden voyages and had careers. Each one could also could behave very differently, and sister-ships built to identical plans could perform in totally contrasting ways once launched and out to sea. Some ships were believed to be lucky and others not. This in turn was linked to the unpredictable element which they plied – the sea. Of course, the varying abilities and fallibilities of the men who commanded them may have played a part.

The majority of surviving figureheads have become detached from their original vessels, which have either been wrecked or broken up. Quite often, the figurehead has been rescued and used for deco-ration or preserved as an historic relic. For example,

HMS *Indefatigable* was a 50-gun sailing frigate built in 1848. In 1864, John Clint, a Liverpool shipowner, set up a charity to look after and educate the orphaned sons of sailors and he bought the *Indefatigable* and had her towed to Liverpool to act as a stationary training ship. By 1912, her oak hull was rotting fast, and she was replaced by a redundant steel light cruiser HMS *Phaeton* which was re-named *Indefatigable*. The figurehead of the old frigate was installed on board this vessel. In the Second World War, the figurehead went with the boys when they were evacuated to North Wales and remained at the shore-based boarding school at Plas Llanfair, Anglesey until it closed in 1995. It had been placed outside near the main entrance to the school and over the years had become fairly rotten but such was the affection for the figurehead among the old boys of the school that it was rescued and restored by some of their practical-minded members. It was then given to the Merseyside Maritime Museum. Although the figurehead had nothing whatsoever to do with the operation of a modern educational establishment, nevertheless it was capable of evoking a strong feeling of affection among its alumni. The same applies to other surviving naval figureheads. They remain honoured pieces in many naval establishments, and they are a reminder to today's sailors that they are heirs to a great tradition which goes back to the days of Nelson and sailing warships. Perhaps today it gets no more than a glance, but in the days when a figurehead went to sea, it was of great importance. It was the ship's mascot, or a talisman – a bringer or receptacle of good luck. Anecdotes from the eighteenth-century sailing navy

testify to the pride a ship's crew took in their figurehead. For example, in 1778 when the Channel Fleet was in full retreat from the French Navy – a disgraceful situation – a boatswain's mate in HMS *Royal George* slipped over her bows with his hammock, which he lashed over the eyes of the figurehead. This was a carving of King George II, who was a courageous man and the last English monarch to personally lead his troops into battle. When challenged about his action, he is said to have replied, 'We ain't ordered to break the old boy's heart, are we? I am sure if he was to turn and see this day's work, not all the patience in heaven would hold him a minute'.

The figureheads on merchant ships in the eighteenth and nineteenth centuries were also a source of pride, although not so much to the crews because

The figurehead of a Maori war canoe. Note the beautifully-carved spirals. (National Museums Liverpool)

A Solomon Islands canoe's distinctive decoration of carved inlaid pieces of mother of pearl. (National Museums Liverpool)

they tended to be a shifting population, signing on for a single voyage aboard a particular ship and then moving on to another ship. But the owners and the captains (and in little ships they were often the same person), took pride in them. It was not uncommon for a wife or favourite daughter to act as a model for the figurehead. Damage or loss of a figurehead was seen as the harbinger of misfortune. For example,

Mr Alfred Worthington, an old sailmaker still working at his craft at the upper Mersey port of Runcorn in 1970, recalled repairing the sails of the schooner *Lochranza Castle* in the 1930s. This little vessel had a particularly beautiful full-length female figurehead, but it had been washed away by the same gale that had torn her sails. Her skipper was distraught and in tears when he told Mr Worthington about his losing 'his lady'. Shortly after the loss of her figurehead, his schooner was wrecked. Perhaps she had run out of luck or perhaps, if you are not superstitious, it was the fact that she was old and strained through carrying heavy cargoes of granite from Ireland to the Mersey.

This kind of superstition about the luck of the ship hints at an ancient origin for figureheads, but there is no consensus among experts about this. The late Philip Thomas in his invaluable *British Figurehead and Ship Carvers* published in 1995 thought they went back to prehistoric times and that perhaps the first heads on the stems of boats were literally the heads of animal or human sacrifices to appease the god of the sea. Peter Norton in *Ship's Figureheads* of 1976 discussed the importance of ritual linked to boats, suggesting that the early boat-builders might have performed ceremonies of the kind carried out by Indian boatbuilders in the late nineteenth century. Norton also pointed out that from the very earliest times, men have decorated and embellished objects not for any functional reason but in order to beautify them for their own sake. It would be natural to transfer this kind of artistic endeavour to boats. By contrast, Frank Bowen writing in the 1930s thought that the origin of the figurehead 'is one of the nautical mysteries, but it goes back far into the past. It seems to have been founded in a mixed desire to conciliate a deity and to terrify an enemy: the idea of decoration probably came later'. The authoritative *Oxford Companion to Ships and the Sea* states that the origin of figureheads 'was probably two fold, a mixture of religious symbolism and the treatment of the ship as a living thing'. So, for example, it stresses the importance of the painted eyes which appear in many maritime cultures, enabling the 'living' ship to see her way across the sea. But eyes were not figure-heads. A J Lewery, an expert on folk art, took

another tack in his *Popular Art Past and Present* of 1991. He thought that figureheads might be traced back as far as the dragons' heads of Viking ships. He saw the figurehead as a separate representation mounted on the bows as a decoration and not the 'soul' of the ship: 'It may later accrue personality or significance, but this was an intellectual investiture by the crew more than inbuilt spiritual belief.' Confused? You can find other authors who have other opinions as well. The fact is that no one knows what motivated the early seafarers to decorate their vessels. Ancient Egypt is the sole exception because this civilisation documented their elaborate religious system in great detail. But for the rest, it is impossible to know. I would also be suspicious of any claims to a continuing tradition of ship decoration passed down the ages. Certainly the ship's eyes appear in various ages and cultures, but as with so many other artistic or technical developments, their use could have started in different places without any connection. A more prosaic explanation for fitting a figure-head in olden times was for recognition. In times when most people were illiterate, signs or symbols could convey vital information. Shops and inns had painted and carved signs, and some of these pictur-esque carvings have been preserved in museums such as the Strangers' Hall Museum, Norwich or the Docklands Museum, London. So, for example, a wool merchant had a carved golden sheep and a nautical instrument seller had a naval officer holding a quadrant. Ships could be recognised in the same way by their distinctive carvings. For example, in the Acts of the Apostles (chapter 28, verse 11) when St Paul was setting off from Malta to Rome, he sailed 'in an Alexandrian ship with the figurehead of the twin gods of Castor and Pollux'.

There are many gaps in the story. First, there is very little evidence before the seventeenth century, and second, figureheads and carvings were in fashion for some cultures and some periods and not others. For example, there were bow carvings of dragons and serpents on Viking ships of the eighth to the twelfth century. But the much larger cogs which followed them did not carry figureheads, even though they had prominent stems suitable for a carving. Ship carvings have been found all around the world and not just in European cultures, many being highly intricate and beautiful. The Arab *baghla* dhow as an artefact of an Islamic culture was not permitted a figurehead and their builders compensated by installing highly carved sterns with beautiful abstract designs. Maori war canoes had stylized human figures that proclaimed defiance to the enemy by sticking out their tongues. They could be either ancestors or gods and were set in a mass of delicate abstract carving based around a spiral. The Solomon Islands canoes had a less flamboyant but nonetheless beautiful type of decoration, consisting of lines of individually carved pieces of mother of pearl on their bows, along the gunwales and round the stern. There are many other examples of carvings and vessel decoration from other cultures. In fact, the idea of decorating your ship to bring luck or to make it look beautiful or recognisable may be pretty well universal. However, what we recognise as a figurehead is a European and latterly a North American tradition. This originated in the sixteenth century with the development of the large ocean-going three-masted ship and particularly with the development of the specialised heavy-gun warship.

Most of the figureheads that survive date from the mid- to late nineteenth century, and these are a tiny proportion of the total number carved. But their earlier development can be traced through plentiful pictorial sources. From the seventeenth century there are many beautiful scale models of sailing warships, and many of these included all the details of their carvings. In some cases there are also miniature models of the figureheads. There was an increasing number of paintings and plans of individual ships which also provide details of ship decoration. Those who commissioned this type of picture usually insisted on a high standard of accuracy and no artistic licence, so we can be reasonably sure that what was on the model or in the painting was true to the full-size version.

Figureheads came in many sizes as well as many shapes. Many but not all reflected the name of the ship. According to at least one nineteenth-century carver's advertisement, it was possible to buy figureheads 'off the peg'. They ranged from a simple head or a bust with the shoulders, to waist height (a demi-figurehead) to three-quarter length down to the calves, to full length down to the feet. More rarely, there are group figureheads. The largest warships of the seventeenth and early eighteenth century were often fitted with a riot of carved allegorical figures. There were also abstract heads; the billet and fiddle heads were common especially in the late nineteenth century. Cartouches or shields might also be fitted which might hold the coat of arms or logo of the ship's owner. But there were also many vessels that did not have a figurehead. For example, many English eighteenth-century collier barks and Scandanavian coasters had straight stems and no bow decoration. However, they might have a small amount of decoration on their sterns.

The figurehead could be part of a wider scheme of decoration, in extreme cases stretching from the bow to the stern. It might also involve painted designs, and in the late Middle Ages much of the latter would be centred around painted sails, elaborate flags and pennants. The high, flat transom stern which was developed in the sixteenth century galleon offered great possibilities for decoration. At first this was largely confined to painted designs, and by the 1620s the stern could be fitted with an array of realistically carved life-size or more than life-size gilded Classical figures. This riot of carving was continued along the sides of the ship with gilded laurel wreaths symbolising victory. From the early eighteenth century, there was a gradual reduction of warship decoration. Merchant ships which were not funded by the state tended have less carvings than warships. At the same time, they tended to follow the fashions of the warship carvers. Nineteenth-century warships and merchant sailing ships were still supplied with some carved decoration, but this was pared down to a figurehead, trailboards and some simple carvings such as ropework and stars around the stern windows. The figurehead remained the essential element. At the end of the nineteenth century the last sailing ships tended to have a simple scroll or coat of arms and not a human figure. Many early steamers had figureheads, and the tradition was perpetuated into the twentieth century by special vessels such as training ships and privately-owned steam yachts. You can still the ghost of a figurehead on some modern ships that carry the company's crest carved or more usually painted on their stems.

It is often the case that when some artefact or tradition becomes rare or goes into decline, popular interest in it is galvanised. This was true for sailing ships. When there were lots of them working, they attracted little attention, but when they were all but gone, they became the subject of popular interest. The only exceptions were the record-breaking clipper ships and the last wooden sailing battleships. From the 1920s when a few four-masted barques still plied the Australia to Europe grain trade, there were many newspaper articles and books about them. Authors such as Basil Lubbock or Keble Chatterton together with new magazines such as *Sea Breezes* (founded 1919) or *Ships and Ship Models* (founded 1931) were dedicated to chronicling the 'Golden Age

The stern carving of a Baghla dhow. (National Museums Liverpool)

of Sail' and the study and collecting of figureheads was part of this trend. It is true that figureheads were always regarded as something special, so you will find that earlier newspaper reports of a ship's launch often will give a detailed description of her figurehead. But when they became detached from their ships, they acquired an added poignancy, and a special aura of nostalgia. This perhaps explains why the figurehead has tended to be treated as something separate from the overall decorative scheme of a ship. This has been reinforced by the fact that later authors have followed the same approach as J Carr Laughton's pioneer book of 1925. He was chiefly concerned about the development of warship carvings. This was probably the correct approach because new developments of style started with state-run navies, but it was at the expense of dealing with merchant ships. As there is such good coverage of warship carving, I have devoted more space to merchant ships' decoration, and have included some of the smaller vessels' ornamentation as well. Earlier books have also tended to see the development of ship carving as separate from developments in the decorative arts ashore and to ignore the economic aspects of the craft. Ship carvers were far from being isolated folk artists chipping away, uninfluenced, in the corner of a shipyard. With the exception of those directly employed by naval dockyards, most were in small businesses mainly working as sub-contractors to shipyards, and many of these firms also turned out all sorts of other kinds of carvings such as wall panels, furniture and picture frames.

There has also been a tendency to use the same illustrations and cover the well-known figureheads. I will certainly refer to some of the favourites but will not necessarily illustrate them, as they can be found in one or other in the many books and articles listed in the Bibliography. Where possible, I have tried to find different pictures and I do not apologise for the fair number examples from the collection at the Merseyside Maritime Museum, Liverpool. After thirty-four years of curating there, it is the collection I know best. I also think that its quality deserves more recognition. I have included photographs of some of the modern replicas of historic vessels because they give a better picture of the overall vessel than the illustrations of the period. There are more British figureheads than those from other nations, but the broad trends in figurehead fashions tended to go beyond national boundaries. Carvings that I regard as typical of their time such as those of HMS *St George*

of 1714 are analysed in some detail. I have redrawn some of the earlier vessels, especially the medieval ones, to leave out the larger-than-life figures and other extraneous details. I have also redrawn figureheads and carvings from paintings or other pictures where they are too small to reproduce properly.

Figureheads are still with us not only as exhibits in museums. There are still wood carvers who carve them. Quite often, the finished carvings become pieces of decoration which are never installed on the bows of a ship. You can also buy replicas of original carvings in a whole range of sizes. Awareness of figureheads is also with us through language. The word 'Figurehead' along with other nautical words and phrases such as 'Splice the main brace', 'Second rate' or 'Son of a gun' have passed into general use. A 'figurehead' is someone who is seen to be in charge and yet has no responsibility. The figurehead has sometimes been seen as having a life of its own because of its human features. For example, Owen Burke's romantic novel *The Figurehead* published in 1979 is about 'Nell Meredith, a young woman of an unusually independent mind for 1855' who on marrying 'is haunted by the sleek and sensual shape of a figurehead whose alien features and alien mind were to challenge and haunt her through all her days . . . '. A figurehead also came to life for a wider audience in a children's television series about the scarecrow Worzel Gummidge. There were two rivals for his affection, Aunt Sally and Saucy Sue who was a figurehead. As Saucy Sue was played by Barbara Windsor, ship's figureheads will be always associated in the English popular imagination with buxom young women.

Galleys to Cogs

This period was not one long continuous development in ship carving. It is simply convenient to cover it all in one chapter because the evidence is spasmodic, and it is essentially a prelude to the European developments from the fifteenth century onwards. One decorative tradition did not necessarily flow into the next. Maritime cultures at different places and periods felt the urge to decorate their vessels. The evolution of floating vessels from simple rafts or boats with paddles to large wooden hulls with sails took place over many centuries. Much of the evidence, especially for the very earliest periods, is scattered and fragmentary, and sometimes contradictory. There are few surviving pieces of written evidence, and much of this is literary. There has been a wealth of archaeological discoveries, but most of these are inorganic materials, which survive better than organic ones, so more often than not this

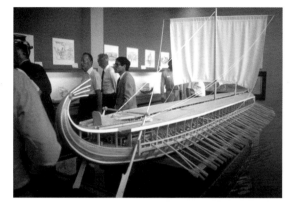

This model of a fourth-century BC Athenian trireme in the Hellenic Maritime Museum, Piraeus, shows the importance of the stern decoration. The bow has eyes and a bronze ram.

means images of ships in stone, clay or metal and not fragments of the actual vessels. This leaves the way open to a wide variety of interpretations because such images are not accurate blueprints. For example, there has been much debate about the precise layout of the Greek triremes with their three banks of oars. To some extent such technical conundrums can be illuminated and sometimes solved by building a replica vessel based on the available evidence, and experimenting with it. Maritime archaeologists have also supplemented the available documentary and archaeological evidence by the study of some more recent types of boats because they appear to incorporate features inherited from ancient craft.

There are a number of features of some ancient vessels which appear to be decorations for ritual or sacrificial purposes. They are drawn from such a wide range of different cultures both in date and place that it is impossible to see a unified tradition.

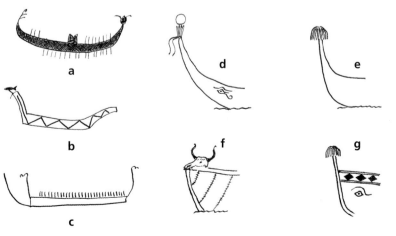

a

b

c

d

e

f

g

Left: Ancient images of boats with animal heads: (a) rock inscription from Nubia about 3000 BC, (b) painting from a 'frying pan' vase from the Greek island of Skyros about 2500 BC, and (c) rock inscription from Bjornstad, Norway about 2000 BC.

Eyes and heads: (d) Ancient Egyptian boat with the papyrus reed ornament topped with the sun symbol of the god Ra and protective eye symbol of the god Horus about 2500 BC, (e) mop head from a painting at St Maria dell'Arco, Naples 1608, (f) Irish sailing curragh 1670, and (g) fishing boat from Villa Real, Portugal, early twentieth century.

Four Roman galley stems: (a) dolphin ram from a mosaic of about AD 200, (b) wild boar carved on a marble basin known only from a sixteenth-century copy, (c) crocodile from one of the galleys at the Battle of Actium, 31 BC, and (d) ram and figurehead from a tomb stone at Ostia about 20 BC.

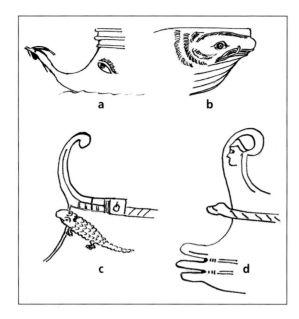

Roman cargo ship of about AD 200 from a tomb stone at Ostia.

Rather, seafaring men, at different times and places, had the same impulse to pay homage to a sea god for a safe passage or to create luck for themselves by carrying a talisman or charm on the boat. The first evidence for boat decoration comes from inscriptions, carvings or painted decoration. These are often difficult to interpret, but they appear to show that once early cultures had got beyond the simple raft or log boat stage, their boats could carry some kind of figurehead or bow ornament. In the Nubian region of Egypt images of boats incised into rocks have been dated to about 3000 BC. They appear to show boats with multiple paddles or oars and a horned animal's head, possibly that of a bull, at the high curved bow and a less prominent ornament on the top of the stern post. Of course, it could be the other way round with the bull's head at the stern. There is no way of knowing. The suggestion is that it was the head of a real animal that had been sacrificed to propitiate the gods and ensure safe voyages but again one can never know. There were similar depictions elsewhere. Rock carvings of boats have been found in Northern Europe, which show boats with animals' heads, which are believed to be depictions of skin-covered vessels dating from the Mesolithic period (8000–6000 BC) to the late Neolithic and the Bronze Age (4000–2500 BC). More recent examples also imply that this sort of bow decoration might represent a sacrifice to the sea gods rather than decoration. James Hornell, who carried out pioneering research on ancient and ethnographic boats, noted actual sacrifices of animals as part of the launching of large sailing ships in southern India in the nineteenth century. The vessel would be ritually cleansed while on the stocks and five sheep would be decapitated, and their heads placed on the bow. He also recorded that in the Solomon Islands it was customary to fix the head of a slaughtered enemy on the prow of a newly-built canoe! He noted

Replica of a third-century BC Greek cargo ship found off Kyrenia, Cyprus, in 1967.

Replica of a third-century BC Greek cargo ship found off Kyrenia, Cyprus, in 1967.

Below: Ship carvings from the Bayeux Tapestry and some later examples of double figurehead ships: (a) William of Normandy's flagship, (b) a painting at Skamstrup church, Denmark 1350–1400, (c) figure-heads from other ships on the Bayeux Tapestry, and (d) the seal of the town of Lübeck 1280, a plain double-ender on the Hedin Cross, Maughold, Isle of Man c.1250, Hebridean galley carving in St Clements, Rodel, Harris 1528.

that in recent times dhow builders of Port Sudan and Djibouti on the East African coast sacrificed a goat before their boats were launched. The skin from the sacrifice was tied to the top of the stem of the dhow as a visible sign that the ritual had taken place. A modified form of this memory of a sacrifice featured on some boats in Christian Europe. A fresco in the church of the Madonna dell'Arco in Naples of 1608 shows a boat with what appears to be a mop tied to the top of the stem. The same device to ensure the good luck of a new boat was found in the Mediterranean at Malta, Sicily and along the Dalmatian coast, and Portuguese fishing boats had a similar device up to the early twentieth century. This might date from pagan times when an actual animal was killed. Many of these fishing boats belonged to isolated communities who were intensely supersti-

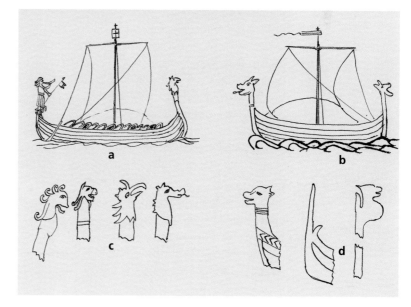

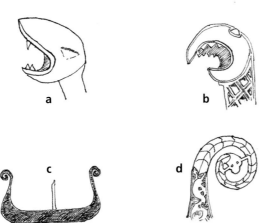

Some Viking ship carvings: (a) and (b) detachable carvings dating from between AD 350 to 400 found in the river Scheldt, (c) Gotland 'picture stone' with serpents at bow and stern of about AD 700, and (d) serpent on the Oseberg ship about AD 800.

tious. There was also the famous sketch of 'A portable Vessel of Wicker ordinarily used by the Wild Irish' by Captain Thomas Philips in 1685. This shows an Irish curragh with a wicker frame with a covering of hides, and the skull and horns of a large ox mounted on the stem. Of course, we have no means of knowing whether this was a common decoration or a unique conceit that Philips had the luck to see and record.

Another early motif was the carving or painting of 'eyes' on the bows of a vessel. Pedantic scholars usually refer to them as *oculi* (Latin for eyes). Painted or carved eyes have been found on the bows of ships throughout the Ancient World, India and China. By 3000 BC in Egypt, boats had an important role in the elaborate funeral rites for the rulers and their nobles, ferrying their mummified bodies and grave goods across the Nile to the necropolis on the west bank. Boats also represented the transition of the soul across to the next world. They were often depicted in wall paintings and carvings and as models left in the graves. One full-size boat was recovered from Cheops' pyramid in 1952, but this was undecorated. Most boats had a carving representing tied bundles of papyrus reed at the top of their stems. This was a reminder that the original

boats on the Nile were made from bundles of such reeds. Some Egyptian boats had the all-seeing eyes of the hawk-headed god Horus painted on their bows as a talisman against evil, and in addition some of them carried a pharaoh's head or symbols of the Egyptian gods such as the sun disc of Ra on the top of their high stems. Although earlier writers have made much of the Egyptians as one of the main roots of ship decoration, most the depictions and models of Ancient Egyptian boats show them without any decoration at all. The eye symbol does seem to have had a hold on many seafarers around the Mediterranean, however, and was still used on fishing vessels around its coasts and along the Portuguese Atlantic coast in the twentieth century. Such was their power on the island of Gozo that anyone damaging a boat's eyes could expect to be killed by its irate and superstitious owner.

Some of the Bronze Age cultures of the Greek islands have left decorated pottery and models of boats powered by paddles with the high bow or stern topped by the symbol of a fish. There have been great arguments among archaeologists as to whether the fish was on the bow or the stern of the vessel, showing the problem of interpreting ancient images from archaeological finds without any other evidence. This problem of determining which was the bow and which was the stern also emphasizes that in many ancient ships the stern could be as important or more important than the bow. By the eighth century BC in Greece large painted bowls called *kraters* were decorated with pictures of long, narrow ships propelled by many oars with large painted eyes on the bow and high curved stern posts. Over time, these 'galleys' increased in size with multiple banks of rowers. They were equipped with heavy cast-bronze rams attached to their bows for attacking enemy warships. The ram and the high curved stern post might also be decorated. Galleys dominated sea warfare in the Mediterranean for centuries. The Romans copied the Greeks and used them in their imperial campaigns from the third century BC onwards, even deploying them to protect the British coast against Saxon and other raiders in the third and fourth centuries AD. Roman carvings such as those on Trajan's column in Rome, on gravestones and mosaics sometimes show galleys with decorated rams and figureheads, with carvings of animals such as eagles, crocodiles or dolphins. These creatures were probably chosen because they symbolized aggression, courage and speed. Some galley figureheads were shown fitted on the end of a horizontal spar projecting in front of the bow. Their Byzantine successors and the medieval Italian merchant city-states such as Genoa and Venice built fleets of galleys as did their main adversary the

Ottoman Empire. Later galleys were equipped with guns, and even in the age of Nelson armed galleys could still offer a formidable threat to sailing warships in calm weather.

The cargo vessels of the Ancient Mediterranean were usually referred to as 'round ships'. This was because they were tubby in comparison with the long, slim proportions of war galleys, built as they were for maximum cargo capacity and not for speed. They were carvel built with a smooth skin of planks fastened edge to edge and their main propulsion was a sail or sails rather than oars. The Kyrenia Ship was a Greek merchant ship wrecked off the Cypriot coast in the late fourth century BC. The cargo and the remains of the hull have been excavated. A replica has been built to test its capacity and sailing characteristics. The builders of *Kyrenia II* took the

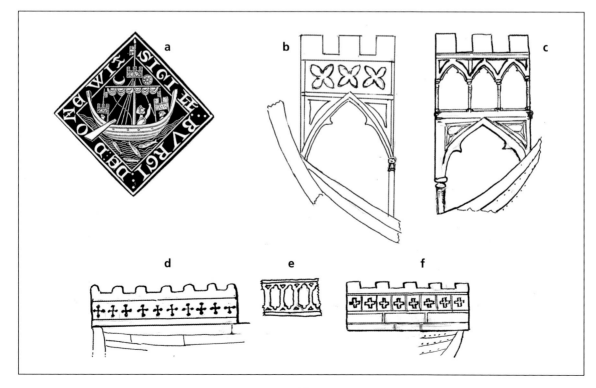

Fore and stern castle decorations: (a) the seal of Dunwich 1199, (b) and (c) fore and stern castles from the Winchelsea seal about 1300, (d) stern castle with cross motif in a manuscript illustration 1330, (e) stern rails from a hulk in Bucci di Lorenzo's painting of St Nicholas rebuking a tempest of 1433, and (f) stern castle with cross motif from the Danzig seal about 1400.

Replica of the cog of 1380 found at Bremen in 1962. Note the battlements around the stern.

World show the stern with more decoration than the bow. This persisted in the war galleys that continued to be the main naval vessel of the Mediterranean for centuries to come. The ram and the bow were sparsely decorated while the stern, which was the place of honour and command, might have carvings and a finely woven or painted canopy.

In Northern Europe around the Baltic, peoples outside the Roman Empire were developing a different type of vessel. They are generally lumped together as 'Viking ships', although in fact there were substantial differences in construction between the Saxon, Viking and the Slavic boats from the eastern end of the Baltic. All these types of boat were built clinker-fashion with the hull planks overlapping and the same pointed shape at the bow and the stern. They were either rowed by a large crew or sailed with a single square sail. They were both seaworthy and shallow-draft. These characteristics made them good for carrying out amphibious raids or carrying cargo to inland trading settlements. Two detached 'Viking' figureheads in the British Museum were dredged up from the River Scheldt. They have been dated to between AD 350 and 400. This makes them contemporary with the increasing raids by the Northerners on the Roman Empire. The older one depicted a serpent and the latter a fierce toothed beast's head with lattice work carving on its neck. There seems to be no doubt that they were made deliberately detachable, corresponding with an old pagan law which required dragon's heads to be unshipped when approaching unfamiliar shores to avoid alarming the local spirits. This perhaps demonstrated the importance of the figurehead as the residence of the spirit of the ship. There were numerous references in contemporary sagas to figureheads. Most of these referred to dragons, and dragons appear on carvings such as the seventh century standing stones on the Swedish island of

trouble to decorate her with eyes. They worked because she made a successful voyage from Greece to Cyprus though admittedly at an average speed of only two knots. The best-known of all the ancient cargo ships were the Roman corn ships that plied between Egypt and Ostia, the port of Rome. This type of cargo ship was also depicted in carvings and mosaics. A gravestone at Ostia of about 20 BC showed the main sail with painted symbols and the stern post carved in the shape of a swan's head, with carving in relief around the stern itself, and figures of Classical gods carved in relief into each side of the stem post. These were probably what was being referred to in the descriptions of the ship with a figurehead of Castor and Pollux in the Acts of the Apostles. There were also two other carved full-length figures of deities at the top of the mast and at the stern. Many of the images from the Ancient

Gotland. There was also the pagan practice of burying their kings and queens in ships. A Viking ship, which contained the probable remains of a queen and one of her attendants, was excavated at Oseberg, Norway in 1904, dated to about AD 815–20. It had a coiled serpent for a figurehead and it is likely that its missing stern had a similar creature. The gunwale running along the top of the hull and the stem itself were also carved in the most elaborate interlaced patterns of dragons.

Viking ships were double-ended and it seems from the surviving evidence that many of them had a carving at the bow and the stern. It became a continuing tradition. The Normans were a warlike Scandinavian people who had created a kingdom in Western France. The famous Bayeux Tapestry, a pictorial account William of Normandy's successful invasion of England in 1066, includes images of some of the ships of the invasion fleet. They were clinker-built double-ended ships with dragons', lions' or eagles' heads on their stem and stern posts. William's flagship was singled out with a lion at the bow and a full-length carving of a man blowing a horn at the stern and a banner with a cross at the top of the mast. Illuminated manuscripts, the seals of towns, wall paintings in churches and carvings all provide further evidence that this form of figurehead continued to be carved for later ships that had inherited the 'Viking' shipbuilding tradition. For example, the seal of the port of Lübeck of 1280 had two dogs. I suspect that many ordinary vessels did not have carvings at all. The double-ended boat with its high stem and stern posts of about 1250 carved on the Hedin Cross at Maughold, Isle of Man was one example. A saint as much as a king might be expected to have a special boat. A wall painting in Skamstrup Church in Denmark of about 1350 depicted a scene from the life of St Olaf. His boat had two animal heads, a dragon at the bow and

possibly a wolf at the stern. The double-headed tradition continued in outlying regions as late as the sixteenth century. The carving of a Hebridean galley in St Clement's church at Rodel on the Isle of Harris depicted a double figurehead. The details have been eroded, but they seem to have been two dragons. This dates from 1528 when Henry VIII on the throne and had a navy of carracks and galleys. Medieval illustrations of ships were not realistic but highly stylised. Monastic manuscripts and images from churches were designed to make theological points and not to provide accurate depictions of contemporary shipping. The figures of saints or crew aboard their boats were out of scale with the hulls. Many seals of port towns and the monarch's naval officers had a ship engraved on them, but the circular form of the seal meant that the ships depicted on them were probably not realistic in their proportions. Once again, you have to be careful in interpreting them.

In the Northern Europe of the later Middle Ages, there were two main types of vessel – the cog and the hulk. The cog was a flat-bottomed, high-sided, decked, clinker-built vessel which was much in evidence in commerce and warfare from the thirteenth to the early fifteenth century. It was particularly associated with the towns of the Hanseatic League of North Germany, a powerful alliance of city states that dominated much of the maritime economy of the North Sea and the Baltic. The cog with its good cargo capacity, high sides for protection against piratical boarders and its cheapness of build was copied by other shipbuilders. They do not appear to have had figureheads. Their use spread southwards and by the early fourteenth century cogs were employed by Mediterranean traders from Catalonia to Venice. The hulk, on the other hand, is not so well documented. It may date back to Anglo-Saxon times because a coin of the tenth-century

English king Athelstan appeared to show a hulk. Hulks appear to have gradually taken over from the cog as the predominant type of vessel in the fourteenth century, but no-one can be certain although the evidence of an increasing number of pictures of hulks and a decreasing number of cog pictures in this century seems to suggest this was the case. Hulks had hulls with highly curved ends, which did not have a stem or a stern post. The detail of the shape and construction of a hulk is unclear to us because no one has found a wreck of one of them. Unlike the cogs, some hulks were shown with figureheads. The often-reproduced carving of a hulk on the font of Winchester Cathedral, which can be dated to about 1180, has a dragon for a figurehead.

Although a figurehead may not have been fitted to all medieval ships, they also appear to have been decorated in other ways. Many of the surviving images of both cogs and hulks show them with fortifications at the bow and the stern. Naval warfare at the time was a variant on land tactics with large numbers of troops embarked. Archery provided the only long-range attack, and capturing a vessel by boarding it rather than sinking it was the usual tactic. The forecastle – a word still in use – and the stern castle together with a fighting platform at the top of the mast provided cover for archers and places of defence in boarding actions. These castles, which were originally temporary additions in time of war, later became permanent structures. Some of the surviving pictorial seals show these were decorated in the same Gothic styles that were found in contemporary churches and castles. The cog on the seal of Dunwich of 1199 (a major East Anglian port that has since been washed away by the sea), showed simply-built castles with tracery and battlements. The ship's castles on the Winchelsea seal of 1284 were supported on moulded columns with decorated tops, and pointed arches. The 'walls' of the castle were be decorated with quatrefoils, four circles set around a larger circle that symbolised either the four main points of the compass, the four Elements or the four rivers of Paradise. The cross, which was the single most important symbol in the Middle Ages, made its appearance on ships' castles. A manuscript illustration of 1330 shows a stern castle decorated with equal-armed crosses modified with balls at the end of each arm. A seal from the town of Danzig of about 1400 had a more conventional square cross and it was also seen in a highly modified form in the painting of a hulk by the Italian Bucci di Lorenzo of 1433.

The other decorative element on medieval ships was heraldic. Knights and their followers had their own particular badges on their surcoats and shields to help recognition in battle. These originally simple insignia developed into an elaborate system of coats of arms, which served as a source of pride, portraying one's antecedents. They were applied to ships in the form of painted shields and sails, flags and pennants. Of first importance was the king's own coat of arms. For example, the seal of the English Office of Admiralty between 1418 and 1426 showed a hulk with a sail painted with the lions of England quartered with the lilies of France. There was a large banner at the stern with the same device and another at the bow with the cross of St George. The seal also showed that the two castles had become part of the structure of the hull and were no longer temporary wartime additions.

The English Admiralty seal of Thomas Beaufort of 1418–26.

Carracks to Galleons

By the fifteenth century a new type of ship called a carrack had developed which was larger and of a different design to the cogs and the hulks and seems to have been a combination of the Northern European and Mediterranean styles of naval architecture. It was built with a substantial set of internal frames which were covered with carvel planking. This innovation made it possible to build bigger and stronger vessels. The carrack was rigged with a combination of the square sails of Northern Europe and the triangular lateen sails of the Mediterranean and usually had three or four masts and a bowsprit projecting over the bow. You can get an impression of a carrack from the replica of Cabot's late fifteenth century ship, the *Matthew* built at Bristol in 1995, although the brass portholes are entirely modern! The forecastle and sterncastle superstructures were integrated into the hull, and in large vessels, which

The modern replica of Cabot's late fifteenth-century carrack the *Matthew*.

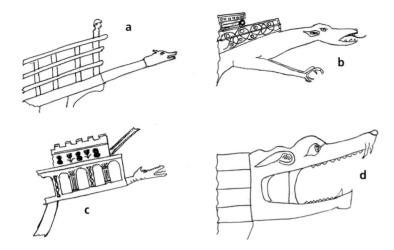

Carrack figureheads: (a) the Mataro ship, (b) the Nuremburg nef, (c) the Burghley nef, and (d) Holbein's drawing of a carrack.

could be up to 1,000 tons, the stern could be as many as three decks high. The carrack had a small figurehead projecting over the bow at angle of between twenty and thirty degrees. This was usually a dragon, a wolf or a salamander. The latter was a kind of wingless lizard which was usually depicted leaping out of a fire, symbolising bravery and courage unquenched by the fires of aggression. However, the relatively small size of these figureheads compared with the forecastle made them look rather insignificant. The only known contemporary model of a carrack has a figurehead of a wolf's head. It is presumed to be a model of a Spanish carrack because it came from the monastery of St Simeon at Mataro, near Barcelona. It has been dated to about 1450 and was probably made as a votive offering for a safe voyage. The model is in the Prins Hendrik Maritime Museum, Rotterdam with later copies in the National Maritime Museum, Greenwich, and the Barcelona Maritime Museum.

The wolf as a figurehead seemed to stay in fashion well into the sixteenth century. A drawing by Hans Holbein dated 1532 showed a small carrack with a figurehead of a wolf with gaping jaws, and an ornamental salt cellar (the Burghley nef) in the shape of a carrack of about the same date also had a wolf. The same type of animal carving could be found on timber houses of the same period. I am particularly fond of a late medieval carving of a wolf with his tongue hanging out which is a corbel on a timber-framed house at Malestroit in Brittany. Turn him through ninety degrees and he could be a figurehead for a carrack! Dragons as figureheads also seem to have been popular, embodying fierceness and aggression like the wolf. Another nef which was in the Nuremberg Museum before the Second World War had a dragon figurehead with outstretched claws. This was probably slightly later than the Mataro model. The engraving of Henry VIII's departure from Dover in 1520 to meet his arch-rival Francis I of France at a chivalric pageant, the Field of the Cloth of Gold, also shows a ship with a figurehead with outstretched claws. Many ships of the period were named after saints, and it would not be surprising if ships thus named carried a figurehead depicting their patron saint. Peter Norton reported seeing (but not illustrating) a painting of a ship dated 1489 with an upright angel as a figurehead in St Mary's Church, Lübeck. If you look at the carved angels that decorate the ends of church hammer-beam roofs in East Anglia, you can see they have the same bold qualities needed for a figurehead. They also project out in much the same way as the figurehead of a carrack.

The sides of the carrack's hull offered opportunities for decoration as well. Contemporary pictures show vessels with a combination of decorative features. The forecastle and poop might be decorated with carved quatrefoils or tracery, while the upper rails often carried a row of shields with coats of arms. This can be seen in the fifteenth century illustrated manuscript known as *The Pageant of Richard Beauchamp, Earl of Warwick*. Dating from

The wolf on a medieval house at Malestroit, Brittany.

about 1485–90, its picture of an English carrack showed a ship with many shields and a wonderful mainsail painted with the Earl's coat of arms. The Burghley nef in the Victoria and Albert Museum, which was made in Paris, incorporated motifs such as Classical pilasters and acanthus leaves which demonstrate the widening influence of the Italian Renaissance and its revival of Greek and Roman designs in the decorative arts. This movement or rather the Baroque style that flowed from it was to have a huge effect on ship decoration in the seventeenth century. Of course, one cannot be sure whether the Burghley nef copied the decoration of real carracks or was a goldsmith's fantasy. The hull was made from a nautilus shell and figures of the legendary lovers Tristan and Isolde sit on the main deck. On the other hand, the layout of the hull and the rigging seem to be accurate.

The use of artillery at sea became common in the fifteenth century. At first, small anti-personnel weapons were mounted high up in the castles, which also had rows of loopholes on each deck for soldiers to shoot arrows or hand guns. After 1500, heavy artillery pieces were mounted in the main body of the hull, firing through gun ports cut through the sides. Such weapons were ship destroyers. This was the beginning of the specialised warship and the change from boarding to broadside naval tactics. In the sixteenth century, however, there continued to be little distinction between large merchant ships and the king's warships, as merchantmen carried guns because piracy was rife, and royal ships were sent on trading voyages in peacetime.

This upper section of a carrack's stern was flat (a transom stern), and this gave space for a new area of heraldic carving. This can be seen in the ships in the painting of Henry VIII's embarkation at Dover in 1520. Again, the risks of relying too much on contemporary illustrations are apparent here. The

Henry VIII's fleet at Dover in 1520. (National Museums Liverpool)

picture, which in any case only survives as a later engraving, was painted twenty-five years after the event, the ships depicted being much larger than the ships that conveyed Henry in 1520. Nevertheless, it provides a good impression of major warships of the English navy in the mid-sixteenth century. The vessel in the foreground has a carving of the royal coat of arms. Her two upper decks have windows and loopholes, and the whole assembly has borders, which might have been carved with some form of moulding, and which are painted in alternating diagonal stripes, which became a prominent feature in ships of the later sixteenth century. The sides of both the forecastle and the sterncastle have semi-circular arches on the lowest deck, then a double row of carved or painted motifs which might have been Tudor roses. At the top there was a continuous row of shields. The engraving was uncoloured and did

A modern reconstruction of the carrack from *The Pageant of Richard Beauchamp.*

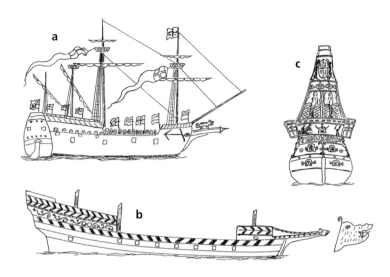

Mid- to late sixteenth-century ship decorations: (a) the carrack *Salamander* from the Anthony Roll, (b) a galleon from the *Fragments of Ancient English Shipwrightry,* and (c) the stern of the *Griffin* from Visscher's engraving.

not show how colourful Tudor ships were. Contemporary records can help. For example, the accounts for the repairs to Henry VII's *Mary Fortune* in 1502 (in the National Archives, Kew), specified that she was to be painted with gold, vermilion, russet, white lead, brown, Spanish white and verdigris (green). Later Tudor vessels were often painted in similar colours with added gold or silver leaf. Perhaps the most striking decoration was not around the hull, but the flags and banners flying from the masts and the yards. For example, Henry VIII's flagship, the *Henri Grace Dieu* of 1514 was equipped with a streamer fifty-one yards long for the top of the main mast, a second one twenty yards long on the fore mast, twenty armorial banners for mounting on the deck with gold and silver embroidery and silk tassels, fifty smaller banners and one hundred small pennants known as 'pencells'. As royal vessels, they not only had to project power by their heavy guns, but they also had to reflect the prestige and majesty of the monarchy. The Tudor dynasty, which had a somewhat shaky title to the throne, took great pains to preserve the mystique of

kingship. The monarchs themselves were always clothed in sumptuous apparel, and they conducted state affairs with pomp and ceremony. This also applied to their ships on state occasions, but there were also long periods when the royal vessels were laid up and neglected for lack of money.

The Anthony Roll, which was compiled by an artillery officer curiously named Anthony Anthony in 1546, provided an illustrated survey of all Henry VIII's ships, their armament and crews. His navy consisted of carracks and smaller vessels such as the rowing barges and galleys. Most of the ships had a long structure projecting from the bow which ended in a spike, probably developed from the ram of a galley. But there is no evidence that it was used for offensive purposes except possibly as a boarding platform. It formed the basis of the bow structure known as the beakhead. The beakhead was to be the base for the figurehead and its attendant carvings in later years. As depicted in the Anthony roll, its only decoration in the mid-sixteenth century was a standing figurehead of a mythical beast such as a salamander, dragon or a unicorn. Anthony's dragon figurehead with its outstretched wings was very similar to the carvings of dragons found in late medieval churches. For example, the porch of Woodbridge parish church in Suffolk has a similar dragon carving. His picture of a galley showed another variation on the figurehead with a carving of a dragon's head projecting over the stern. His drawings show how gaudy these Tudor ships were with a predominance of red and yellow, and like the 1520 engraving every vessel flew long streamers and many banners.

The carrack survived into the second half of the sixteenth century. The ponderous hull made it a good but slow bulk carrier, and the Portuguese continued to use huge ones of over 1,500 tons to convey precious goods from the Orient, as their large size and high sides provided protection against pirates and enemy vessels. They had much the same decorative scheme as Henry VIII's ships. For naval warfare and many merchant adventures especially exploration expeditions, the galleon became the vessel of choice. It is not clear how the design developed but it certainly owed something to the fast and manoeuvrable Spanish and Portuguese caravels of the late fifteenth century and also to their cargo-

carrying naos and their galleys. A Portuguese trading caravel was illustrated in a manuscript from Dordrecht in the Netherlands dated 1572. This was clearly quite a large vessel with twenty-four guns in her main armament. She had a narrow beakhead and no figurehead. There were painted chevrons on the forecastle and the poop as well as some painted shields. When fitted with a combination of square and lateen sails rather than just lateens, they proved

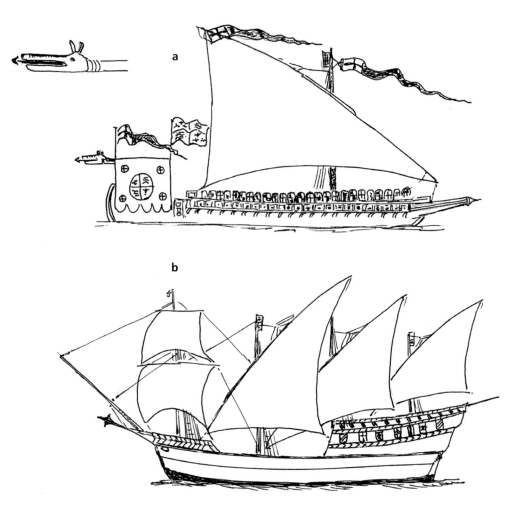

a

b

(a) One of Henry VIII's galleys from the Anthony Roll, and (b) a Portuguese caravel from a Dutch manuscript of 1572.

The replica of the *Golden Hind.*

to be excellent vessels for long ocean voyages. The galleon was built with broader proportions than the caravel and a very strong hull. They had a kind of crescent-shaped profile with a beakhead projecting forward of the bow, a low forecastle (unlike the carrack) and a half deck, quarterdeck and possibly a poop stepped up from the main mast. They also tended to have two decks above the waterline on which to mount cannon. Increased speed and ease of manoeuvre meant that battles could be fought between ships at longer ranges, and the need for castles with large numbers of soldiers to repel boarders was reduced. The galleon was adopted by most seafaring nations, but their designs and uses varied considerably. Spanish ones were exclusively warships. The Portuguese galleons were also warships which were much smaller than their great carracks. The Dutch on the other hand had strongly-built galleons called pinnas and more lightly-built bulk carriers known as fluits.

The decoration of all these galleons relied mainly on paint rather than carving. In the famous panoramic painting of the English fleet attacking the Spanish Armada in 1588, it is difficult to tell the two protagonists apart except for their different flags. The manuscript *Fragments of Ancient English Shipwrightry* of 1586 has coloured drawings which show the decorations of some of the Elizabethan galleons. These were brightly painted in stripes and geometric designs either in red and green; yellow, red and black or black and white (rather like the black and white stripes or chevrons so fashionable as a house decoration in the same era). The specification for repainting the *Elizabeth Jonas* when she was rebuilt in 1598 consisted of 'New painting and gilding her beakhead on both sides with her majesty's whole arms and supporters; for painting the forecastle; the cubbridge heads on the waist, the outsides from stem to stern; for like painting and new gilding both the galleries with Her Majesty's arms and supporters on both sides, the stern new painted with divers devices and beasts with fine gold'. The 'cubbridge heads' were probably carvings where the forecastle and the quarterdeck were stepped down to meet the waist. These were later known as hances and carvings were fitted there in the seventeenth century. There seems to have been a small figure at the end of the galleon's beakhead. If anything the figurehead had an even less prominent position than on the earlier carracks where at least it projected clear of the rest of the ship. The *Fragments* also showed two different kinds of figurehead. There was a figurehead of a boar's head right on the end of the beakhead, and there was a small upright animal head sticking up from it. The replica of Sir Francis Drake's *Golden Hind* gives a good idea of the overall paint-scheme of a late Tudor ship and of a typical figurehead – an upright carving of a deer's head. Jansz Visscher's engravings of Lord Howard's ship

the *White Bear* in 1588 had a small standing bear. However, as Visscher engraved his prints long after 1588, there must be some doubt about this picture's authenticity. The galleon era continued on into the early seventeenth century and paintings from the early 1600s show a more elaborate kind of standing figurehead. The *Royal Prince* of 1610, seen on part of a larger painting of 1618 in the National Maritime Museum, Greenwich, had a knight on horseback with a bracket behind him carrying a crowned helmet. A painting by the Dutch artist Cornelius Verbreeck of an English galleon of the 1620s has a leaping lion with a globe on his head. This was an early example of a motif that was to become universal for warships. It is also noticeable that he was fitted on the end of the beakhead and not on top of it. Most of the later figureheads were to be fitted in this position. This painting was sold at Christies some years ago and I have not been able to trace it, but it is illustrated in Michael Leek's *The Art of Nautical Illustration*.

Galleons of all nationalities seemed to have carried a carved device on their transom sterns, which might reflect the name of the ship or be the coat of arms of its owner. A Visscher engraving of the *Griffin* shows a stern where the royal coat of arms has been pushed up to the top of the stern with a band of 'strapwork' below. The open gallery which jutted out from the stern and the quarters was a new feature which had probably developed from the small 'necessary houses' (lavatories) seen on either quarter of the carrack's stern and became another opportunity for decoration. Its supporting brackets and its sides might be carved and painted. The gallery and the spaces between the windows of the great cabin on the *Griffin* have carvings of what appear to be allegorical figures. Other European galleons appear to have followed the same trend to more elaborate carving around the stern. For example a late sixteenth-century Danish church ship model of a galleon which was owned by Trinity House at Leith had painted carvings in low relief along the side of the hull and its two stern galleries. This was a foretaste of the great 'theatrical stage' that the sterns of major warships became in the seventeenth century.

The galley continued to serve as the main warship in the Mediterranean, much as it had done since Classical times. The main protagonists were the Ottoman Empire and Holy Roman Emperor and his allies, chiefly Venice and Spain. The expansionist policies of the Ottoman sultans were bitterly opposed by the Christian powers. Naval campaigns in the sixteenth century culminated in the great battle of Lepanto in 1571, where the Turks were decisively defeated. The sixteenth-century galley had a single bank of oars and two triangular lateen sails, and several guns in the bows as well as smaller swivel guns. The ram was retained not as an offensive weapon in itself but as a boarding platform for assaulting enemy vessels, and in the case of the Venetian galleys, there was a lion's face on its tip. The sides of the forecastle and the stern might have shields and the pavilion at the stern for the officers usually had a canopy over it with a large armorial design painted on it. Big streamers flying from the yards were also common. Another type of Mediterranean warship was the galleass, a combination of sailing vessel and galley, which had a deck of guns above its banks of oars. They were used by the Venetians and the Genoese for trading as well as warfare and there were several in the Spanish Armada. Like most other warships of the period their hull decoration was mainly paintwork. Their predominant colours were yellow and red, and they also carried many heraldic shields.

Merchant ships of the sixteenth century seem to have followed the same kind of decorative schemes as the royal ships but on a lesser scale. The distinc-

tion between types of ship was blurred as we have already seen, private owners, especially noblemen, might own warships. They could be use them for trade, licensed piracy – privateering – or in the monarch's service in return for a fee. For example, Sir Walter Raleigh had the very large 50-gun *Ark Raleigh* built in 1587. He then sold her to Elizabeth I who had her renamed *Ark Royal* and made her the flagship of the English fleet that defeated the Spanish Armada in 1588. A contemporary woodcut shows her to be a galleon with guns on two decks with a flower motif painted between the gun ports and geometric motifs taken from heraldry such as chequers and diagonal bars on her upper works. The smaller merchant vessels and fishing craft were unlikely to have had figureheads but may have had simple painted decoration.

(a) Figurehead from the *Royal Prince* 1610, and (b) the lion from an English galleon painted by Verbeeck about 1620.

CHAPTER 4

Warship Carvings in the Baroque Era

By the end of the sixteenth century, the galleon had become the principal warship of all the European naval powers, although in the tideless Baltic and Mediterranean the galley was still important. The sailing battleship and its smaller companions – frigates and sloops – were the main components of all European and American navies down to the beginnings of steam power in the mid-nineteenth century.

Naval competition between the European nation states intensified, and wars were fuelled by religious and national rivalries. The Ottoman Empire, particularly the semi-independent Barbary States of North Africa, remained a threat in the Mediterranean. There were tensions over trade and colonies. Spain, the first colonial power in the Americas, suffered from other countries threatening its dominance. The Dutch Republic had become a major mercantile power, which competed with the French and the British for colonies or trading stations in North America, India and the East and West Indies. In 1600, England was a second-rate naval power; by 1700, it had become the most powerful naval force in Europe. Increasing tonnage of traditional imports such as spices and textiles from the East and new commodities such as sugar, rum and tobacco (and the

attendant slave trade for providing labour in the plantations) all expanded commercial maritime activity at an unprecedented rate.

Some leading seventeenth-century monarchs, including Charles I, attempted to strengthen their position by claiming, and in Charles' case believing, that they were appointed by God to rule. Louis XIV (1638–1715) of France was the prime example. He was the Sun King – *le roi soleil* – always demanding deference, always seen in magnificent surroundings, keeping his turbulent nobility at court and recruiting able administrators to execute his orders. He expanded the French Navy and its principal ships were decorated in the utmost carved splendour to reflect the power and glory of their master. Tsar Peter the Great (1672–1725) did the same in Russia. He built a new capital of St Petersburg and equipped himself with a navy to gain control of the Baltic. This boosting of kingliness brought with it huge expenditure on decorating buildings and all the monarch's possessions including his navy. A king's warships were to project power at sea and to act as floating statements of royal prestige, and so warships of the seventeenth and early eighteenth century became the most lavishly-decorated ever launched.

They were decorated in a fashion that was

Middle: Cesare Ripa's image of 'Virtue' 1603.

different from the designs of their predecessors, inspired by artistic developments ashore. Some of the old heraldic elements such as the royal coat of arms and emblems were combined with a whole range of new motifs. The latter emerged from the artistic developments collectively termed the Renaissance, the rebirth of interest in the heritage of Greece and Rome in literature, architecture and the pictorial arts. Evidence of this Classical influence can be traced back to fourteenth-century Italy. There was a rediscovery of realism in painting, sculpting the human body and the development of techniques such as perspective. For the decorative arts such as carving, there was also the development of characteristic patterns, which could be repeated and elaborated to cover flat surfaces in a highly ornamental way. Architecture adopted the Classical principles of proportion and symmetry. These Italian artistic developments were spread gradually to other parts of Europe by travelling artists and through illustrated books of architectural and ornamental details. These books contained examples of decorative detail such as Classical caryatids (carved figures acting as supporters of a building), pediments, acanthus leaf scrolls and 'grotesques' – strange beasts in repeating patterns inspired by Roman wall paintings found underground (in grottoes) in Rome. There were also compilations of Classical mythology and symbols. The most influential of the latter was *Iconologia or Moral Emblems* by Cesare Ripa published in 1593. The second edition of 1603 was an illustrated dictionary of virtues, vices and other abstractions from 'Abundance' to 'Zeal' presented as male or female personifications adorned with symbolic objects. 'Virtue' for example was an Amazonian female in armour on a winged horse spearing a Chimera – a

Right: A modern model of the Royal Yacht *Mary* of 1660. (National Museums Liverpool)

Far right: The *Mary's* stern. (National Museums Liverpool)

mythological monster with a goat's head, a lion's body and a serpent's tail.

Ripa's work was part of an artistic movement that developed from the Renaissance known as Baroque. Characterised by exuberant decoration and expansive curving forms, it began to spread from Italy at the end of the sixteenth century. Carvers both of naval and merchant figureheads used many of the motifs that had been devised during the Baroque era, though often in diluted form. Figures or busts in Classical dress were a useful shorthand by which a carver could depict a ship's name with an abstract quality such as 'Hope' or a deity or ancient hero such as Venus or Achilles. Artistic innovation started at the top at royal courts, the church or through patronage of rich business-

Above: One of the lions supporting the royal coat of arms. (Swedish National Maritime Museums)

Above left: The *Vasa's* stern. (Hans Hammarskiold)

An early seventeenth-century nobleman from the *Vasa's* stern. (Swedish National Maritime Museums)

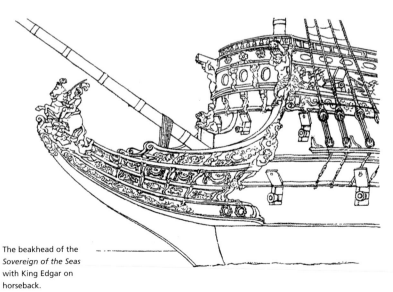

The beakhead of the *Sovereign of the Seas* with King Edgar on horseback.

men, and gradually filtered down through society. Some features were retained and others rejected. This was why pattern books and pictures of symbols were important sources of inspiration. Artists would not blindly copy the images, but took away what appealed to them or what suited a particular commission. However, the innate conservatism of the maritime world meant that once some decorative feature was adopted, it remained in use for a long time. So, for example, rolling acanthus leaves carved in relief made excellent supporting decoration on warships. They were then adopted in a simplified form for merchant ships.

From the early seventeenth century, the sources available for charting the development of ship carving become more plentiful. A few full-size examples survive as well, including the Swedish *Vasa* of 1628 which was salvaged with most of her carvings intact. Other underwater sites have yielded smaller fragments of carving such as a cherub carved in relief from the small warship *Swan* wrecked in 1653 at Duart, Scotland. There are also some notable survivals of whole sections of carvings from warships such as those from the stern of the French galley *Grande Reale* of 1690 in the Musée de la Marine, Paris or the English coat of arms from the *Royal Prince* captured by the Dutch in 1667, and displayed in the Rijksmuseum, Amsterdam. From the late seventeenth century we also find plans of warships preserved in state archives, and these include designs for figureheads and decoration. Perhaps the most important collection is that held at the Musée de la Marine in Paris. Many European monarchs or their ministers took a detailed interest in proposals for new ships. The result was the construction of scale models, which made it easier for laymen to appreciate the shape and appearance of the proposed vessel. The British ones, which are known as Navy Board models, were probably built from the

Navy Board model of
HMS *Neptune* of 1683.
(National Museums
Liverpool)

century Dutch painters were the first to develop a distinct school of marine painting, producing seascapes, naval battles and portraits of individual ships. They also influenced painters in other countries.

In the sixteenth century, many warships were also armed merchant vessels and even royal ships could be sent out on trading voyages, but the later big, heavily-armed two- or three-decked battleship was too valuable a military asset for other uses. Their building and maintenance required the concentration of a skilled and dedicated workforce with facilities such as dry docks and warehousing for materials. Warships spent long periods out of service, as there were no winter campaigns until the end of the seventeenth century. Dockyard employees sometimes included carvers, but carving could also be sub-contracted out. There was a considerable increase in size of major warships. The Swedish *Vasa* of 1628 displaced 1,300 tons and had sixty-four guns, but the French *Royal Louis* built at Toulon in 1664 displaced 2,000 tons with 120 guns. First Rates were the largest warships, usually serving as admirals' flagships and were lavished with the most decoration. However, most units of the battle fleet were smaller Second and Third Rates of between seventy-four and ninety-eight guns. Below them there were Fourth to Sixth Rate frigates and sloops. These acted as scouting, patrol and despatch vessels. All of these ships were provided with a figurehead and stern carvings.

This period also saw the development of a more scientific approach to ship design and construction. Builders used plans instead of relying on handed-down formulae for the correct proportions. Building so large a wooden floating structure as a battleship was a complex task, which had to reconcile many conflicting requirements. The hull had to be seaworthy and manoeuvrable, at the same time as

early seventeenth century. The oldest surviving model of a named ship is that of the 80- to 86-gun *Naseby* of 1655 (renamed *Royal Charles* on the restoration of the monarchy in 1660). Such models were built to the highest standard and included their decorative schemes in full detail. There are also many paintings, drawings and prints. Seventeenth-

being a stable gun platform, with sufficient space to accommodate the large crew and their stores. It also had to be strong enough to withstand damage. Not every master shipwright got it right. The most celebrated disaster was the *Vasa*, which capsized on her maiden voyage in 1628. There was an increasing literature on ship design and most of these works, such as Nicholas Witsen's book *Architectura Navalis et Regimen Nauticum* published at Amsterdam in 1671, were concerned with warships.

At the beginning of the seventeenth century, the long low beakhead of the galleon was still the main feature of a warship's bow. It provided an anchoring point for the bowsprit, an angled spar projecting in front of the ship which carried two sails and was lashed down to the beakhead by the gammoning rope. The platform in the centre of the beakhead provided a convenient 'place of ease' for the crew. The low position of the beakhead was a drawback in heavy weather because it would scoop up water rather than throwing it aside, and thus was vulnerable to damage. By the 1640s, it was being constructed in a

The replica of the Russian frigate *Shtandart* of 1703.

Vasa's lion figurehead as salvaged in 1962. (Swedish National Maritime Museums)

shorter, more compact and upright form. The high structure of the stern was also lowered and widened compared with that of the galleon and the galleries at the stern of the vessel where the officers were housed were partly or wholly closed in. This made the quarter galleries, which stuck out on each side of the stern, look rather like the projecting oriel windows of a house. The largest warships were built with three gun decks, and both the size and number of guns were progressively increased. There were also a series of improvements to the rigging, sails and other features such as the method of steering.

The figurehead became a part of the beakhead supported by carving in relief on the structural parts of the head itself and on the forward bulkhead (wall) of the forecastle. The decorative scheme for the stern was elaborated with the royal coat of arms at the top on the taffrail. This presided over a theatrical array of large realistic allegorical figures trumpeting the glory of their monarch. The taste for realistic carvings of heraldic animals and Classical deities was not simply a nautical fashion. It was also found in large new aristocratic homes and royal palaces. For example, Knole and Hatfield House in England, completed in about 1605 and 1612 respectively, have wonderful carved staircases with newel posts ornamented with standing cupids and lions. The lion was the single most important motif. Derived from the heraldry of the Middle Ages, the king of beasts symbolized strength and agility, and thus royal power. He was adopted by many European rulers except those within the Holy Roman Empire where the eagle, the king of birds, was the prime symbol of power. He was found on the ships of the Spanish, Dutch, Danish, Swedish and Russian navies. The Royal Navy fitted him on ships below First Rate. He thrived among all the welter of cupids and grotesques as a leaping or 'salient' figure in heraldic terms. The *Vasa*'s lion figurehead was a fierce creature with open jaws and glaring eyes. He had two lion companions on the stern supporting the royal coat of arms. The rest of the stern's decorative scheme consisted another fifty-eight carvings. Those on either side of the stern quarters were more than twice life-size. The carvers working on the *Vasa*'s decoration had produced figures which were both realistic and fantastic. The lions have an exaggerated fierceness with heavily incised and stylised features, ensuring they would be visible at a distance. On the other hand the human figures, though dressed in exotic armour, have faces which seem to have been carved from life. It is undoubtedly the largest and finest surviving piece of ship carving, and is completely 'over the top' in the way only the Baroque style can achieve.

The British *Sovereign of the Seas* was another vessel intended to represent monarchial power. It also supported the legitimacy of the Stuart dynasty's claim to the throne in which the carvings had a narrative role. Although she was a powerful warship armed with 100 guns, she was also a symbol of English naval power and the prestige of Charles I, who wanted the biggest and most finely-decorated warship in the world. Laid down in 1635, she took the combined resources of the Deptford and Woolwich dockyards to complete her by 1637. She cost over £40,000, and this included £6,691 for her decoration. This latter amount paid for an overall scheme of gilded carving running from the beakhead to the stern along the topsides including the bulkheads of the forecastle, the quarterdeck and the poop – the uppermost deck at the stern. It was a carefully worked out set of allegories glorifying the monarchy. The rider on the beakhead was the Anglo-Saxon King Edgar trampling down seven kings – 'the first who could truely write himself the absolute Monarch of this Island . . . and whatsoever his sacred majesty [Charles I] challengeth concerning his absolute dominion over the four seas, hee justly claimeth from this King Edgar, being his true lawful hereditary Successor'. Thomas Heywood, who wrote that in 1637, went on to describe many of the other carvings and to explain their symbolism. There was a cupid bestriding a lion on the beakhead towards the forecastle 'which importeth that sufferance may curb Insolence and Innocence restraine violence', which in turn was an allusion to the merciful nature of Charles I. Behind that there were six pilasters along the bulkhead carved to represent 'Counsell' (wisdom), 'Care', 'Industry', 'Strength', 'Virtue' and 'Victory'. The figure of 'Care', for example, was carved holding a compass. When taken together all these elements led to 'Victory' which was represented holding a laurel wreath. There were more carved figures at the hances of the waist, the points at which the rail was stepped down from the forecastle and the quarterdeck. Here, there were images of Classical gods such as Jupiter, Mars and Neptune. At the stern, there was the winged figure of Victory, arms outstretched, supported on each side by Jason, the first of the Argonauts and Hercules. There was yet more supporting carving, and painted on the lower section of the stern was the following:

'He who Seas, Windes and Navies doth protect
Great Charles, thy great Ship in her course direct'

By the mid-seventeenth century there was a trend to raise the angle of the beakhead and shorten it. The beakhead on the Royal Yacht *Mary* of 1660 was an example of an intermediate stage in this development. The *Mary* had been built for the Dutch East India Company, and was presented to Charles II by the wealthy city of Amsterdam on his restoration to the English throne in 1660. The *Mary* was a Dutch type of shallow-draft singled-masted yacht. Yachts of this period were built for pleasure cruising and as naval despatch vessels. After a short time in royal service, she became a government despatch vessel ferrying mail and officials across the Irish Sea until she was wrecked off Holyhead in 1675. Although her wreck was discovered in 1971 and many interesting finds were recovered, including her bronze guns, none of her carvings have survived. A contemporary pen-and-ink sketch by Willem van de Velde has been used to build a model of her. She had a splendid unicorn figurehead standing above the beakhead in a similar position to King Edgar on the *Sovereign of the Seas*. Warships built within a decade of the *Mary* had upright figureheads, which were integrated into the beakhead and the stem post. The *Mary* had carved and gilded scrollwork down the beakhead and along the sides of the quarterdeck. Laurel wreaths (a symbol of victory) surrounded the gun ports. The skylight on the main deck and the great cabin aft had pilasters elaborately carved with grotesques. On the stern the royal coat of arms was supported below and either side by a whole mass of carved figures including two very large ones on each

quarter. Above the coat of arms, on the taffrail there is the badge of the city of Amsterdam flanked by two gilded supporting figures, and three gilded lanterns.

This carving scheme could be found on both large and small warships of the late seventeenth century. It embraced not only the outer end of the hull but the upper sides including gun ports, the entry port on to the main deck, the forecastle, quarterdeck and poop bulkheads, belfry, timbers such as bits for holding ropes and catheads for hoisting the anchor. The beakhead continued to be shortened and raised so that the figurehead took on an upright pose. The Navy Board model of the 90-gun HMS *Neptune* of 1683 has a crowned lion figurehead which is vertically positioned with his back legs astride the stempost. The beakhead had been built to a standard layout which started in the mid-1660s. It consisted of a horizontal head rail with two or three more rails below them, all with mouldings. There were five vertical head timbers carved with grotesques and another five grotesques as pilasters across the forecastle bulkhead. The knightheads, which were structural timbers which projected above the fore end of the forecastle, were topped with turbaned male heads. The catheads for handling the anchors and their supporting brackets were also carved, the outer end of the cathead had a carving of a lion's head. This pleasing and punning carving was perpetuated in later warships and merchant vessels. The barque *Garland* was fitted with an iron casting of a lion's head as late as 1865. There were carvings at the changes of level along the hull, and laurel wreaths around the upper gun ports. This was only a Second Rate warship! The carvings on the replica of the Russian frigate *Shtandart* of 1703 are an example of how a smaller warship might be decorated. The lion figurehead, the grotesques and the laurel wreaths are all prominent.

Charles I's flagship the
Sovereign of the Seas of
1637.

Warship carvings reflected their nationality, the personal tastes of the monarch, and the skills of the carvers. The French statesman Jean Baptiste Colbert (1619–83) was appointed Minister of the Marine by Louis XIV in 1669. He built up the French Navy and the new ships he commissioned were decorated in a manner appropriate to the Sun King. He employed decorative artists schooled in the Baroque style to supervise the design of new carvings for ships. He also established schools of carving in the French dockyards. The French carvings tended to be technically more proficient and adhered more to the Classical rules of proportion and symmetry than other nations' carvers. English carvers seemed anxious to cram all possible ornament into every available space. In the decorative arts, the French were the international arbiters of fashion, and they initiated the Rococo style which was lighter and more elegant than the Baroque. This new style was often assymetrical and abstract with shell and coral-like forms and lots of 'C' and 'S'-shaped curves. This can be seen in the early eighteenth century engravings of the sterns of a French warship and a galley.

fig. 1.

fig. 2.

French designs for the stern for a three-decker warship and a galley of the early eighteenth century.

CHAPTER 5

Eighteenth- and Nineteenth-Century Warships

Naval warfare between the European powers continued throughout the eighteenth century, starting with the War of the Spanish Succession and culminating in the Revolutionary and Napoleonic Wars from 1793 to 1815. The American War of Independence (1776–83) also resulted in the creation of a new naval power, the United States of America. Throughout there were shifting alliances, but the principal antagonists were France and Britain. Shortly after 1815, the South American colonies of Spain and Portugal broke away to form their own independent republics, build navies and fight amongst themselves.

Tastes in decorative art also changed over the

Right: The bow of HMS *St George* 1714. (National Museums Liverpool)

Far right: Close-up of the figurehead of HMS *St George*. (National Museums Liverpool)

century. The exuberance of the Baroque era in its final Rococo form was gradually overhauled in different places and different times by a revival of Classical restraint and discipline particularly during the second part of the century. This applied to warships as well. The whole-hull schemes of gilded fancy work of around 1700 were gradually reduced as a matter of economy as well as of taste. There were also changes in the construction of warships. Ships increased in size. HMS *Victory* of 1765, the only surviving First Rate, measured 226 feet in length and 52 feet in the beam with a displacement of 3,500 tons. Copper sheathing to protect the hull from marine growth and borers such as the Teredo worm was introduced in the 1770s. The appearance of warships also changed over the century, the overall profile becoming flatter and the beakhead shorter and higher until it was finally phased out in favour

of the round bow. This trend started on smaller ships, and was subsequently applied to larger ships. The round bow was shorter and built right up to the top of the forecastle, making ships drier in a head sea and improved the number of guns that could brought to bear on an enemy that was being pursued. The figurehead was also no longer mounted astride the stem post in that rather awkward leaning-back position. As most figureheads were busts, they were faired into the two trail boards behind them. The rails of the head which had carried so much ornament a century earlier were often reduced to no more than two horizontals and three verticals which had rounded mouldings cut by a plane rather a carver's gouge. The traditional transom design of the stern meant that no guns could be mounted there to defend the ship from an attack in the rear, so 'circular' and elliptical designs

Left: The Red Lion at Martlesham, Suffolk.

Far left: The stern of HMS *St George*. (National Museums Liverpool)

Above left: Figurehead of the Swedish *Aron* 1784 at Karlskrona Naval Museum. (J Kearon)

Above middle: Figurehead of the Swedish frigate *Camilla* 1785 at Karlskrona Naval Museum. (J Kearon)

Above right: HMS *Victory's* rebuilt stern of 1802.

of stern were introduced in to the Royal Navy from 1821 and these allowed for the mounting of stern-firing guns. The building of wooden warships continued into the 1850s and some were equipped with auxiliary steam propulsion, but they were finally rendered obsolete by the increasing efficiency of explosive shells, the rapidly improving technology of constructing hulls from wrought iron, increasingly powerful steam engines and screw propellers.

Sources of information on eighteenth-century figureheads are plentiful. Contemporary technical publications included chapters on figureheads and ornaments, and plans of individual ships or classes of ship also become much more common. The

British Admiralty collection has been catalogued up to 1889 in the late David Lyon's *Sailing Navy List* and his posthumous *Sail and Steam Navy List*. Some individual contracts for figureheads survive as well. There are equivalent collections in other nation's naval archives. Detailed models, which included the decorations, continued to be commissioned until 1793 when wartime pressures caused most of them to be replaced by much simpler ones. There are also a few surviving detailed models of figureheads including a fine collection of model figureheads fashioned in wax in the Naval Museum at Copenhagen. Many fine paintings and images in other media of eighteenth-century warships have

also survived. A few later examples of sailing warships have been preserved including Nelson's flagship HMS *Victory*, and several frigates such as the American *Constitution* of 1797, the British *Foudroyant* of 1817 and *Unicorn* of 1824 and the Portuguese *Dom Fernaando II e Gloria* of 1843. There are also many more surviving figureheads.

HMS *St George* completed in 1714 was a typical First Rate of early eighteenth century. Built seventy-seven years after the *Sovereign of the Seas*, the symbols and the extensive decoration were still in fashion. The Navy Board model of the *St George* is in the collection of the Lady Lever Art Gallery at Port Sunlight, Merseyside. It is not as well known as the

Navy Board models in the National Maritime Museum, but it is of equal quality and is different from the models that have featured in earlier books on figureheads. The first thing to notice is how the beakhead has been raised and shortened compared with *Sovereign of the Seas*. It has a horse and rider for a figurehead – St George instead of King Edgar. The horse, a wild stallion with a curly mane, is rearing up on its hind legs astride the stem with his armed rider to starboard. St George is wearing the scale armour, the short kilt of a Roman legionary (not the full suit of medieval armour in which he was usually portrayed) and an unfeasibly large plume on his helmet. On the port side his oval shield (incorrect

Above: Portuguese galley *Bergantim Real* 1778. (Portuguese National Maritime Museum, Lisbon)

Above left: HMS *Victory*'s 1802 figurehead.

for a Roman) carries the royal coat of arms within a belt and topped by a crown. The whole composition rests on a curved line of acanthus leaves. The rest of the beakhead is decorated in a much less ostentatious fashion than ships of twenty or thirty years earlier. The head timbers and the forecastle

bulkhead have been cleared of pilasters representing human or animal grotesques, becoming instead an exercise in Classical architecture which relies on its proportions and Classical details. The main element is a series of fluted pilasters of the Roman Doric order of columns, reflecting the gradual move back

The lion in Sutherland's Shipbuilder's Assistant, 1711.

Koefoed's Danish lion 1783.

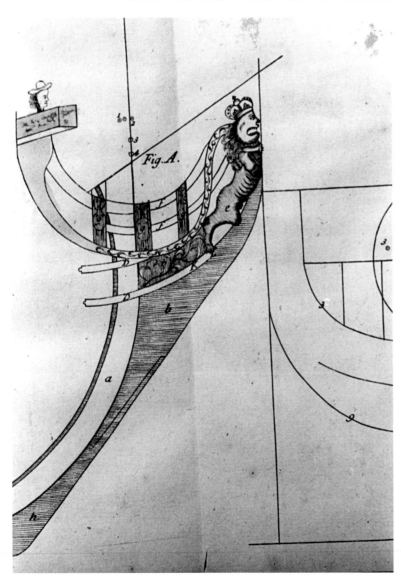

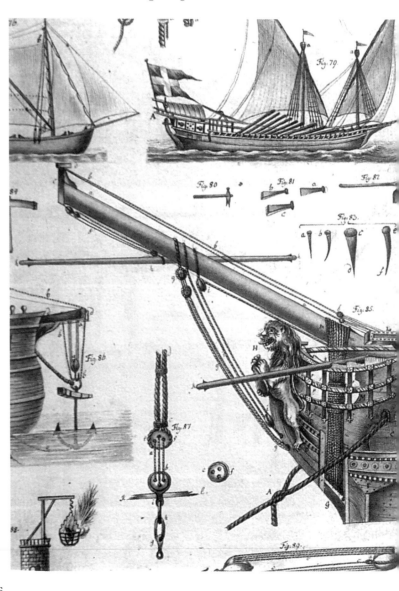

HMS *Camperdown's* figurehead of the goddess Isis 1819. (Tay Division RNR)

to a more austere, less florid style of architecture for houses and churches which was beginning to become fashionable in Britain at this time. It was based on a revival of interest in the strict adherence to Classical rules as propounded by the Italian architect Palladio (1508–80). It also reflected the growing concern of the naval administration at the cost of ship carvings.

The wreathed gun ports have disappeared except for six on either side of the quarterdeck. At the stern, there are three galleries rather than the two of earlier vessels. The upper two have walkways. All three are an integrated design, which wraps around the quarters. The older kind of projecting 'oriel windows' have disappeared. On the stern proper it is the carvings on the taffrail that dominate. The royal coat of arms has disappeared and has been replaced by a classical scene of triumph. A Roman soldier has his back to the spoils of war – cannon and spears – and in the centre a female figure symbolizing Victory is being driven in a four-wheeled chariot pulled by a lion and a horse. This composition is supported on each side by two leaning figures; the one to port holds a grotesque mask and that to starboard has the badge of St George. The galleries are much more restrained with turned balusters on the upper one and the windows separated by more Doric pilasters. The lower walkway and the space below the lower closed-in gallery have painted decoration and this includes mermaids holding the royal monogram and Neptune being driven in a sort of sled drawn by winged horses with fishy tails. There are also some dragons thrown in as well.

The lion continued to be the most common figurehead. Some had a changed appearance being three-quarter length and clutching a shield in their fore paws, while others had a stylised curly mane, which gave them a rather Chinese look. Perhaps this can be attributed to

the popularity of Rococo designs, which incorporated Chinese decorative elements. The Red Lion pub at Martlesham, Suffolk, has one of the few surviving early eighteenth-century lion figureheads, which has these characteristics. The lion appeared in textbooks of naval architecture. For example, William Sutherland's *The*

Above: HMS *Unicorn's* modern figurehead. (Unicorn Preservation Society)

Far left: HMS *Diana's* figurehead of 1822. (Chatham Historic Naval Dockyard Trust)

HMS *Hastings's* figurehead of 1818. (National Museums Liverpool)

Shipbuilder's Assistant, which went to press in 1711 included a diagram of how to set out the proportions of a lion figurehead. As late as the 1780s maritime encyclopedias by Falconer and the Danish naval officer Georg Koefoed included a lion, but by then the use of the lion was steadily declining in favour of more individual figureheads. In 1727 the Navy Board first permitted smaller warships to have figureheads which were not lions. From that point, ships of all rates tended to be fitted with figureheads that had some reference to their names.

The apogee of elaborate carved decorative schemes was probably reached about 1700. But there was mounting concern about their cost. Back in the 1680s, James II had issued a directive to reduce costs, but this seems to have been ignored. Both the master shipwrights who supervised new building and ships' commanders were reluctant to give up the carved finery of their charges. By 1700, the costs of carved work on a First Rate battleship of one hundred guns or more amounted to £896, a Second Rate (ninety to ninety-eight guns) was just half that sum and a Third Rate (sixty-four to eighty guns) was between £293 and £164, and the Sixth, lowest Rate with between twenty and twenty-eight guns cost £52 to £42. In 1703, the Navy Board decided it had to impose some restrictions and ordered that carved work should be reduced to a figurehead and trailboards at the bow, and the taffrail and the two figures on each quarter with all the surrounding woodwork with only simple mouldings at the stern. At some point gold leaf was largely replaced by gold paint, but nevertheless extremely elaborate figureheads for First Rates remained the fashion well into the 1750s.

French naval carving took a similar path. But the training of 'sculptors in wood' rather than mere ship carvers made for a better standard of design. They also adhered far closer to the rules of Classical

sculpture. William Falconer in his *Universal Dictionary of the Marine* of 1780 contrasted the differing approaches of the two great rival navies: 'The head of a ship however has not always an immediate relation to its name, at least in the British Navy . . . Hence we sometimes observe the head of Jason supplied by Medea, or a beast of prey made the representative of an illustrious lady. The same liberty of design may therefore with equal propriety, be allowed to symbolize the success of our arms by a group of heterogeneous figures, of sundry shapes and sizes, according to the artist's opinion of their superiority or subordination. Their attitude and situation, as well as their size, must accordingly depend, in great measure, on the space into which they are to be crowded; for although the figures may be of equal importance in themselves, yet as there is not room for all, as large as life on a ship's head, it becomes expedient to diminish a few, in order to give place to others . . . The heads of many of our ships of war have undoubtedly great beauty; and candour must acknowledge that some of the most elegant and judicious have been borrowed from the French, which are never left to the invention of illiterate mechanics. If there be any rule to determine the subjects and quantity of sculpture employed in ship-building, it seems to be connected with the ideas of dignity and simplicity . . . It seems hardly possible for us to recollect the various disasters to which a single hero, or goddess is exposed by tempestuous weather, battle, or the unexpected encounter of ships, without trembling for the havoc and indecency that may happen to an assemblage of gods, conc-shells, princesses and satyrs; heroes, blunder-busses, sea-monsters, little children, globes and thunder-bolts, and all the apparatus necessary to constitute the head of a ship of the first class in our navy.' Falconer's polemical criticism was directed against the elaborate figureheads of the HMS *St George* kind. These had continued to be commissioned for British First Rates. For example, Nelson's last flagship, HMS *Victory* of 1765, had a huge one eighteen feet high with a bust of King George III surrounded by allegorical figures. However, by the 1780s First Rates were only a small component of the British battle fleet. Second and Third Rates especially the 74-gun two-deckers were the mainstay of the Royal Navy's battle line and usually had single figureheads.

The French approach also influenced other continental navies. The Portuguese royal galley, the *Bergantim Real* of 1778, has a sea dragon figurehead which could well have been French in design. However, the time of such elaborations was passing, and single figures in Classical dress, often austerely painted white, came into favour. These might be busts or full standing figures, and some particularly notable examples were carved by Johann Törnström, the master carver to the Swedish Navy who was trained by a Frenchman working at Stockholm. They were full-length figures with streaming drapery and dynamic arm gestures. There is a fine collection of his work displayed at the Swedish naval dockyard at Karlskrona. The 60-gun *Aron* of 1784 had a figurehead of a well muscled male holding aloft a wreath of victory, having only the remains of a cloak and some drapery over his private parts to protect him in the chilly Baltic. In other words, he had all the characteristics of a Classical Greek sculpture of a warrior. The figurehead from the frigate *Camilla* completed the following year is equally dramatic in its gesture, holding up an arrow with its point close to her exposed bosom. This dramatic gestures of Törnström's figureheads were the stock-in-trade of the fine art sculptors of the period. For example, Matthew Wyatt's memorial figure to Princess Charlotte at St George's Chapel, Windsor, of 1817 holds the same pose as the figurehead of the *Aron*.

Stern decoration went through a gradual

reduction from carvings across the whole width to carvings confined to each quarter. The stern of French 80-gun *Duguay-Trouin*, which was captured at the Battle of Trafalgar in 1805 and renamed HMS *Implacable*, is on display at the National Maritime Museum, Greenwich. This a plain design with Classical pilasters between the windows, a dummy gallery with turned balusters between the upper and lower cabins and an S-shaped leaf carving topped by oak leaves on each quarter. After her rebuilding in 1802, HMS *Victory*'s stern was equally restrained; there were three tiers of windows separated by two rows of turned balusters and no open galleries. On each quarter there was some simple scrollwork which incorporated a small figure in relief midway and a carved bracket at the bottom. Above this, the taffrail was outlined by a simple moulding surmounted by the Prince of Wales' feathers and spears, standards and other war trophies

In 1796, the Admiralty issued an order that all figureheads were to be replaced by billet heads. The result can be seem in HMS *Victory*'s figurehead which was replaced the 1765 one in 1802. This was the royal coat of arms supported by only two cupids costing only £50. The majority of new ships continued to be fitted with figureheads, but the quality of the carving varied because most of them were contracted out to commercial firms and the budget for carving was by then heavily restricted. The official allocation for a Third Rate was £21, for a frigate £6 and for a sloop £3. Single figurehead busts usually reflecting the name became the norm although there were the occasional reminder of past glories such as that of HMS *Nelson* of 1814, which had an eponymous bust supported by large figures of Fame and Britannia. According to Peter Norton, the dockyard carvers retained their skills for the first two decades of the nineteenth century. From 1809 a special class was introduced at the Portsmouth Naval

Academy to teach the best of the apprentice ship-wrights mathematics and other theoretical aspects of their work. The subjects included drawing, which it was hoped would assist them to design figureheads, but there was never a large take-up of the places and the course was eventually scrapped in the 1830s. By then most carved work was contracted out. The most important contractors were the Hellyer family of London. The earliest reference to them was a quotation for a new figurehead for the 38-gun Fifth Rate HMS *Phoenix* of 1783. By 1810, they appeared to have been in regular receipt of orders, and from 1830 to about 1860, they were the main carvers to the Royal Navy, and from the surviving records, they supplied carved work for at least 234 vessels, but the quality of the work varied. The anatomy of many of their carvings was somewhat suspect, with many of their figureheads having stiff extended necks. Also, the carving of the draperies around their waist was often in sharp cuts rather than subtly folded. But the work was done to a price. HMS *Camperdown*'s figure-head is an 'excellent' example. This female, which is preserved at the Tay Division of the Royal Naval Reserve, is a female Amazon peering out from under a large Greek helmet with roughly-modelled scale armour and a very coarsely-carved cloak and tunic. Her bosom looks like rather like one of the singer Madonna's costumes of the 1980s. She was supposed to be the Egyptian goddess Isis for a 60-gun vessel completed in 1819. She was supplied by Messrs. Grayfoot and Overton for the low price (and you can tell!) of £20 16s. Another example is the figurehead of the frigate HMS *Diana* which was carved in 1822 by George Williams, who held the contract to supply Chatham Dockyard. In the late Philip Thomas's words: 'It is hard to associate this stolid figure with the goddess of the hunt'! However, some good-quality figureheads from this period have survived as well. The 74-gun Third Rate HMS *Hastings* was built in Bombay in 1818, but her figurehead was carved in England. It is a finely-modeled portrait of Warren Hastings with the facial detail anatomically correct, but it has the feeling of austerity because it was painted white with only a few gilded trimmings on the epaulettes and lapels of the uniform.

The spare elegance of HMS Victory's stern was perpetuated in later designs. The other major decorative feature of the rebuilt Victory was the striking paint treatment of the sides of her hull; they were painted in broad bands of yellow and black with the gun port lids picked out in black in a kind of chequer board pattern. Later vessels had white bands instead of yellow, like the 24-gun frigate HMS Unicorn of 1824 which is preserved at Dundee. She has a round bow with a figurehead of a unicorn, which has no more supporting decoration than the trail boards which have moulded borders outlined with yellow paint. Incidentally, as the Unicorn was never commissioned and remained a stationary training ship, she was never fitted with a figurehead. The unicorn she carries today is a modern carving, which is however true to the period. Her stern is almost plain except for her name painted on a blue ribbon below between two lines of gold paint with another above the commander's cabin windows and a single carved badge above them.

Other navies did not suffer the same deterioration in quality. The French Navy also adopted the round bow about the same time as the Royal Navy, but continued to produce well-carved figures although they were busts rather than full-length. Surviving figureheads from other navies such as those of Spain, Naples and the northern Italian states suggest that there were fine carvers still at work. The figurehead carvers of the new United States of America were influenced by French carvers such as Jean Antoine Houdon, who had been commissioned to carve a statue of George Washington in 1792. The bust for the USS George Washington of 1817 by Salomon Willard was almost a copy of Houdon's piece. However, most of the US Navy's ships were small and were only fitted with simple billet heads.

Wooden sailing battleships were still being constructed as late as 1853. HMS James Watt launched at Pembroke Dock in that year had no more than a simple white painted bust of the great pioneer of steam mounted on a billet head. But maritime traditions were slow to change and figureheads and carved decoration persisted into the era of steam ships, although on a much more limited scale.

The launch of HMS James Watt in 1853.

Later Merchant Sailing Ships

By 1600 the ocean-going merchant ship was becoming a separate type of vessel from the warship, although the process was slow and merchant ships continued to be hired as small warships, naval transports or carried their own guns for protection or privateering for the next two centuries. Their decoration, though always less extravagant than that of warships, tended to follow the same trends. By the mid-nineteenth century, some merchant ships attained an unsurpassed size, speed and beauty. But it was a beauty achieved by line and proportion and not by prodigious amounts of carving. By 1900, very few new sailing ships were being built and the existing fleet gradually dwindled through wreck, war and the breaker's yard. A few remained as sail training ships or static museum ships.

Ships increased in size as trade continued to expand and more distant routes were opened up. About 1600, the average merchant ship had a cargo capacity of under 200 tons, but by 1800 average cargo capacity had probably doubled. Some of the last sailing merchant ships built from the 1880s onwards were massive, carrying as much as 5,000 tons of cargo. The three-masted ship rig remained the standard for deep sea ships, but the length of the masts and the number of sails increased. The profile of the hull changed. In 1600 merchant ships had low beakheads and high sterns, but over two centuries this profile gradually flattened out. The bows changed in shape and the flat transom stern changed to a round counter. The proportions of hulls also changed, ships becoming much longer and proportionately narrower

Left: The beakhead of a Dutch East Indiaman about 1620. (National Museums Liverpool)

Far left: The stern of a Dutch East Indiaman about 1620. (National Museums Liverpool)

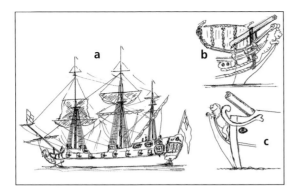

Left: Mid- to late eighteenth-century figureheads: (a) *King George* from a Liverpool ship bowl, (b) Dutch East Indiaman *Meermin,* (c) Liverpool West Indiaman *Watt,* (d) gammon knee figurehead of privateer *Viper,* (e) French merchant ship 1781, and (f) Falmouth Packet *Duke of Marlborough.*

Far left: Seventeenth-century merchant ships: (a) Liverpool West Indiaman 1682, (b) London ship *Loyal George* 1664, and (c) Basque whaler 1675.

Merchant ship model of about 1750. (National Museums Liverpool)

in the beam. Speed in sailing ships was a function of length as well as shape, and from the 1840s through to about 1870, there was a demand for fast sailing ships for carrying premium freights such as tea from China and gold from California. The most important change was that from wood to iron which began in the 1840s. Very few large ocean-going wooden ships were built after 1860 except in North America. Steamers took over the most profitable trades from about the 1870s, and sailing ships were confined to carrying mainly bulk cargoes such as coal and grain and were given less and less decoration.

No merchant-ship figureheads seem to have survived from the seventeenth century except for the dubious Golden Cherub figurehead in the collection on the Cutty Sark which is said to date from 1660. There are a few from the late eighteenth century, but there are hundreds of survivors from about the mid-nineteenth century. A few late nineteenth-century wooden vessels have been saved and over twenty iron or steel ones have been preserved. Models of merchant ships are less common than warships, although after 1800, the number of surviving models increased. Many were half models, used both for designing the ship and for display. As a ship's hull was symmetrical about its centreline, it was only necessary to show one half of the hull for design purposes. Some of these half models were fitted with miniature figureheads. Illustrations of merchant ships also became more plentiful in the eighteenth century, with portraits of individual vessels became increasingly popular from the 1770s. Technical works were published which covered both naval and merchant ships. For example, the Swedish naval architect F H Chapman's *Architectura Navalis Mercatoria* of 1768 included details of figureheads and stern carvings in the plans. Shipbuilder's plans have survived from the late eighteenth century and some of these show the proposed

Above: Liverpool slave ship by William Jackson about 1780. (National Museums Liverpool)

Above right: Close-up of the female figurehead astride the stempost.

figurehead and carvings for the ship. A few nineteenth-century ship carvers' sketchbooks have also been preserved.

Early seventeenth-century English vessels followed the design of their Elizabethan predecessors with their small or non-existent figureheads and geometric painted decoration. The most common cargo ship of this century was the fluit – a low-cost bulk carrier of Dutch design. The East Indiamen were the most prominent merchant ships until the early nineteenth century. The main companies were the English, France and the Dutch all founded around 1600 with an exclusive right to trade with India, China and the East Indies – long-distance routes with many hazards. These ships were well armed and looked like a Third Rate warship even though they usually only carried one deck of guns. All were highly decorated, partly a reflection of their prestige and partly as camouflage. If an East Indiaman could pass herself off as a warship, then the risk of pirate attack could be reduced. The bow of an early seventeenth-century Dutch East

Indiaman had a long beakhead with a lion, 'strapwork' and grotesque pilasters for its head timbers and soldiers' heads carved on the knightheads which supported the inner end of the bowsprit. The stern had bulging quarter galleries and a huge Baroque shield with the coat of arms of the city of Amsterdam as its main carving. All later East Indiamen followed the fashion in naval carving for the next two centuries. Examples of this include three contemporary models of East Indiamen in the Rijks Museum, Amsterdam, dating from 1649, 1721 and 1740 respectively, and a plan of the Swedish East Indiaman *Sophia Albertina* of 1753. These are all fitted with lion figureheads. Later models such as those of the British *Scaleby Castle* of 1798 and *General Grant* of 1810, in the National Maritime Museum, Greenwich were fitted with single busts and two broad white-painted bands around the hull in imitation of a 74-gun battleship.

Most ship owners either were private individuals or syndicates with unlimited liability. They faced the harsh economic reality of making a profit by

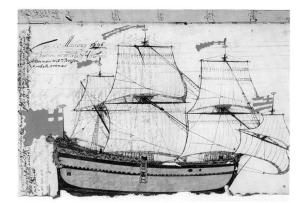

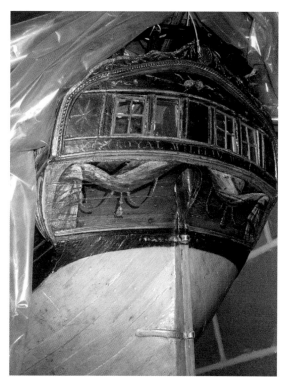

Far left above:
The English fluit
Mulberry. (Lancashire
Record Office)

Far left below: Neptune
Inn, Ipswich, window
bracket.

Left: Royal William stern,
early nineteenth century.
Note the theatrical
curtains. (Glasgow
Transport Museum)

carrying less exotic cargoes with much competition and many hazards. Nevertheless, many owners took a pride in the appearance of their ships and would decorate them according to their means and the fashion of the time. A lion seems to have become a standard merchant-ship figurehead until the second half of the eighteenth century. Again, this may have a form of camouflage, since a merchant ship with a lion could at first glance be taken for a frigate or a sloop. Some examples of this include a drawing in a private collection by Willem van de Velde of 1664 of the London ship *Loyal George*, an engraving of a Basque whaler of about the same date in the Spanish Naval Museum, Madrid and a painting of Liverpool in 1682 with several West India or North American traders anchored in Merseyside Maritime Museum. My latest sighting of a lion is in an engraving of the first dock at Liverpool by Rooker of 1770.

By the middle of the eighteenth century individual figureheads were becoming popular. A rare contemporary model dating to 1750 has a sea

horse, and the plan of the Dutch East Indiaman *Meermin* of 1760 illustrated in David Macgregor's first volume on merchant sailing ships showed a mermaid. Chapman in 1768 also had two plans of merchant frigates with full-length female figures astride the stem posts. A painting of a Liverpool slave ship of 1780 showed a similar figurehead, while that of a captured French West Indiaman of 1781 had a waist-length figurehead of a Classical warrior.

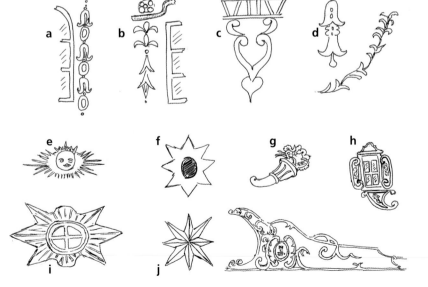

It seems likely that late eighteenth-century French merchant ships had more elaborate figureheads than other nations. The National Maritime Museum, Greenwich, has one of a fashionably dressed woman where the details of her outfit are carved with great precision, even including the lace on the sleeves of her dress. Another late eighteenth and early nineteenth-century variation was a ship with a straight stem and a gammon knee (a bracket) projecting from the stem post. Its main function was to act as a tying-down point for the gammoning rope around the bowsprit and it could also carry a carving in relief or a small figurehead. The Liverpool privateer *Viper* in a painting by Joseph Parry, dated 1781, had a snake's head at the end of her gammon knee.

Many seventeenth- and eighteenth-century Dutch, Scandinavian and Mediterranean ships, and the English collier barks from the North East, had no figureheads but often had decoration on their top sides, sterns and their quarters. The English fluit *Mulberry* of about 1690 had a painted or carved wave decoration along the sides of her forecastle and quarterdeck. The stern and quarter galleries had their own importance because they accommodated the master, officers and high-status passengers. Vital recognition information – the ship's name and home

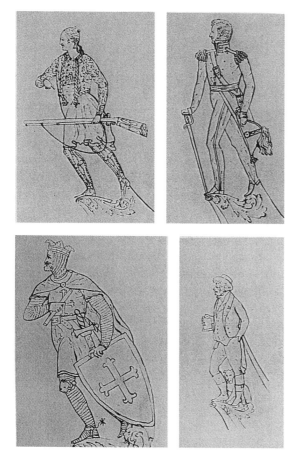

Far left: Designs for figureheads by R Lee of Liverpool, early nineteenth century.

Left: Full-length figurehead of Plenty, Ceres or Demeter. (Tyne and Wear Museums Service)

port – also formed part of the stern's decorative scheme. In the early seventeenth century the stern narrowed above the stern windows and this taffrail area was used for carved emblems or figures in relief. This feature was retained as the main stern carving. It was often linked with carvings on either quarter and its subject could range from a single image, to a pair of leaning figures or leafy tendrils supporting a central badge or shield. The carvings between the windows were almost abstract motifs such as 'drops' – a vertical line of shapes such as a chain of bell-shaped flowers. Sometimes, the ship's name was reflected in the stern carvings. In 1747, Thomas

Johnson carved a lion figurehead for the new privateer *Jenny* and 'a figure of Miss Jenny, with a white rose in her breast' for the stern. The *Royal William*, a model of the early 1800s at the Glasgow Transport Museum, had a carved taffrail with a badge at the centre, trophies of war below and stars on each side of the windows. There was a pair of painted stage curtains below the windows. This unusual motif was probably taken from warships' stern decoration.

Smaller ships had simpler decorations such as a single line of carved rope to enclose the name, or a star or similar badge on either side. The stern

Right: Nanny the Witch on the *Cutty Sark*, 1869. (Cutty Sark Trust)

Below right: The headless *Ambassador*, 1869.

Below: The eponymous figurehead of William Turner, 1833. (National Museums Liverpool)

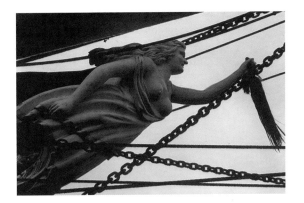

carving of *William Miles* of 1816 in the collection of the Bristol Industrial Museum is another fine example, with the name painted on a carved drapery hung over an oar. The merchant ships' stern galleries had their own decorations with carved supporting brackets, pilasters between the windows, and metal sheathing laid in the form of scale armour on the curved roof. A seventeenth-century merchant ship's quarter gallery brackets would have been similar to those on the upper windows of the Neptune Inn, Ipswich, which date from 1639. On some smaller vessels, the gallery was reduced to no more than a window with a carved surround.

From the 1790s the beakhead began to be shortened and made higher. The horizontal head rails were reduced to two and the height between them reduced, and the vertical head timbers were reduced to three or abolished altogether, the open space above them often being filled in. The trailboard between the upper and lower cheeks at the base of the beakhead took on an important role. It began carry more carvings from the base of the figurehead towards the main part of the hull. This had the pleasing effect of visually integrating the figurehead with the rest of the hull. They were often beautiful in their own right. The usual motif was some kind of foliage such as laurels as a symbol of victory, oak leaves as a symbol of strength, acanthus and thistle leaves as symbols of life, immortality and punishment or vine leaves with grapes as symbols of plenty. These leaf forms were frequently carved in Rococo style with C and S-shapes, diverging leaves and elongated stems. The West Indiaman *Watt* of 1797, which was an early example of this reduced head, had a half- or waist-length female figurehead and vine leaves and grapes on her trailboards.

The tendency to austerity and economy in warship carvings was reflected in the mercantile world in the substitution of a billet or a fiddlehead

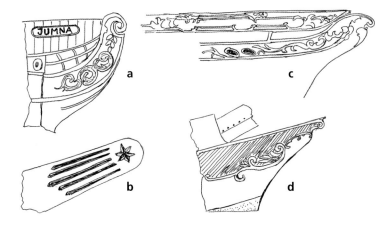

Left: Plainer figureheads:
(a) *Jumna* 1833, (b)
Comet 1854, (c) *Fiery
Cross* 1859, and (d)
Archibald Russell 1905.

Below: Eagle sternboard
from the American ship
Jane wrecked in 1840.
(National Museums
Liverpool)

as three dragons, a unicorn, an osprey, an alligator, Neptune and one gammon knee head. Bristol was an important port and this survey may be typical of the rest of the British Isles.

While the bust remained the most popular form, there also seems to have been a growing number of standing figureheads. Their stance had been changed from the awkward astride and upright position to standing on a step in the stem post and leaning forward at an angle of about seventy-five to eighty degrees. R Stewart-Brown's *Liverpool Ships in the Eighteenth Century* included pictures of standing figureheads of a Red Indian with a musket, a cavalry officer, a medieval knight and a John Bull figure clutching a tankard. These were taken from a book of drawings by the Liverpool ship carver R Lee. From their subjects and their style, these were drawn in the early nineteenth century probably after 1820. Unfortunately, nothing is known about Lee and his book, which was privately owned, has disappeared. It

for a figurehead. The former originated with the volute, the spiral scroll of an Ionic column. It pointed downwards, while its companion, the fiddlehead (from the spiral on a violin's head) pointed upwards. The Liverpool brig *King George* of about 1760 had an interesting and early combination of a bust of a sea horse above a fiddlehead, while a model of the Falmouth Packet *Duke of Marlborough* of 1806 had a simple billethead. The Whitehaven ship *Jumna* of 1833 had a billet head combined with her name on a panel and curvaceous carving on the trailboards, but these examples may have been exceptions. The head and shoulders bust in a vertical position was probably the most popular form of figurehead in the early nineteenth century. The published transcripts of the Ship Registers of Bristol between 1814 and 1838 for ships over 150 tons provide details of the figureheads. Out of a total of 232 ships, the majority – 159 or 69 per cent – had busts. Of these, forty-four were identified as women, nineteen as men and the rest were not specified. There were thirty-seven ships without figureheads and the rest were 'figureheads', billet and fiddle heads with a few unusual ones such

Elephant stern carving from the *Marco Polo* 1851. (Prince Edward Island Museum)

is also impossible to discover the name and date of the ships for which these designs were carved, but there are plenty of standing figureheads still in existence to confirm that Lee was following a fashion. Good examples include the figure of Plenty at Tyne and Wear Museums, the *William Turner* at Merseyside Maritime Museum, the *Caledonia* in Morwenstow churchyard and the figure of a Greek warrior on the Tantons Hotel, Bideford. Mystic Seaport Museum, Connecticut, also has an excellent collection of American standing figureheads. It was clearly a popular design with American ship carvers, and many of their prestigious clipper ships of the 1850s carried standing figureheads. The Aberdeen (or

clipper) bow introduced in 1839 had a raking stem without head rails and the hull at the water line had much finer shape than in earlier ships. This form of bow became popular for fast sailing vessels and was perpetuated in the later iron and steel ships. The tea clipper *Cutty Sark* is the best surviving example.

Nineteenth-century ships tended to have figureheads that were linked to their name, and if not the second choice seems to have been a female bust or waist-length carving. Some figurehead carvers supplied ships from stock. The Americans tended to opt for an eagle or a billet head. The latter was found on other nations' ships such as the Dutch and the French. Some of the French clippers had a

Stern of the *Sigyn* 1887.

popular. The figurehead of the tea clipper *Cutty Sark* is of Nanny the Witch reaching out to grab the tail of Tam O'Shanter's horse at the climax of Robert Burns' popular poem. She is a beautiful young woman in her 'cutty sark', literally a short shirt. Female figureheads with one or both breasts exposed were not uncommon in spite of alleged Victorian prudishness. Other female figureheads wore the fashions of their day and it is possible to date some figureheads according to their costume. Many of these survivors have lost their identity, but look as if they were portraits of owners' wives or daughters.

Male figureheads could also be in Classical dress to represent abstract qualities, or the heroes and battles of ancient Greece and Rome. Uniformed figures could be either actual military heroes or represent generic types such as *Fusilier* or *Rifleman*. The headless figurehead of the clipper *Ambassador* of 1869, preserved by the Patagonian Institute at Punta Arenas, Chile, is a good example. This fine waist-length piece depicts a diplomat in full uniform complete with gold epaulettes and blue sash across his chest. Rather than carve the top of a prosaic pair of trousers, the carver has swathed the lower part in toga-like drapery which must have merged neatly into the trailboard carving. In a less cynical age, ships could be named after politicians. The *Cutty Sark*'s collection includes figureheads of Abraham Lincoln, William Gladstone and William Wilberforce. This trio were perhaps more admirable than most, but other, more controversial figures had ships named after them. The owner might commission a portrait of himself. The *William Turner*'s standing figurehead is of a gentleman, and is almost certainly a portrait of the Belfast merchant William Turner. His outfit with a white neckcloth, a dark blue double-breasted tailcoat and tight trousers of a contrasting colour with straps under his boots was fashionable in 1833, the year his ship was

shield surrounded by pretty Rococo carving. Ship's names changed from 1800 to 1850. At the beginning of the century there seems to have been a preponderance of Christian names especially female ones. They could be single such as *Elizabeth* or *Mary*, or with surnames or two names together such as *John and Mary*. By 1850, there was a greater number of Classical names (*Achilles*, *Neptune* etc), abstract qualities such as *Faith* or *Electricity* and literary or military heroes such as *Ivanhoe* or *Wellington*. Perhaps more shipowners had received a Classical education at public school. Abstract virtues were often carved as female in Classical draperies. Tyne and Wear Museums have an unidentified full-length female carrying a wreath of ears of corn and fruit and a basket fruit in her right hand, suggesting she represented Plenty, the Roman goddess Ceres or her Greek equivalent Demeter. Geographical names could also be represented by females often in Classical garb. Poetic names such as *Witch of the Wave* or *Coral Nymph* had to be female too. Literary heroines such as *Titania* or *Guinivere* were also

Stern of the *Cutty Sark* 1869. (Cutty Sark Trust)

launched. James Baines was a Liverpool shipowner who was noted both for his vanity and his flair for publicity, and in 1854, he sat for William Dodd who carved a full-length figurehead for his latest clipper that was being built at Boston. It was packed up and shipped across the Atlantic to be fitted on the 2,515-ton *James Baines*. But not all clippers had standing figureheads. The American *Comet* of 1854 had a knee with a star and rays incised into it, and the British tea clipper *Fiery Cross* of 1859 had a billet head and a shield and a much extended leaf and strap work along the head rail and the trailboards.

Animals and birds were less common. The bird which was the subject of most carvings was undoubtedly the eagle. There must have been hundreds of eagles carved in the early nineteenth century for the growing American mercantile marine, based on the bald eagle, which was one the major symbols of their republic. Many of these bird carvings were sternboards, which were positioned at the taffrail above the main cabin windows. They were carved with outstretched wings, and often clutched a shield with the stars and stripes painted on it with a scroll in their beaks with the nation's motto '*e pluribus unum*'. The stern carving of the American ship *Jane* which was wrecked off the coast of North Wales in 1840 is a very good example of this. Canadian shipbuilders were at their most productive

The bow of the *Majestic* 1875. (National Museums and Galleries of Northern Ireland, Ulster Folk and Transport Museum)

in the 1850s and the stern carvings of the Australian emigrant ship *Marco Polo* of 1851 departed from the formulaic stern decorations of drops and stars, consisting of two figures, one in Oriental dress and one in a European suit separated by an elephant. This famous vessel was not the only ship to have carved stern figures, another good example being from the German ship *Sleipner* in the Sunderland Volunteer Lifesaving Association's headquarters. By the mid-nineteenth century most carved work on the stern tended to be consist of one curved board of curling foliage with a central shield or boss. This can be seen on the wooden barque *Sigyn* of 1887 which is preserved at Abo, Finland, and which has residual bits of the older gallery carvings on each quarter as well. The elaborate carvings on the stern of the Dundee ship *Corona* of 1866 show how older forms were retained. Like the *Sigyn,* she had carvings on each quarter as a last trace of the quarter gallery carvings. Their form followed Rococo motifs supporting a central shield. The central carving of the stern was another shield supported by war trophies, and this again harked back to common motifs for warships of the seventeenth and eighteenth centuries.

Until the mid-nineteenth century ships' sterns had remained broad, slightly curved and dominated by the cabin windows. The round or elliptical counter stern was developed with the introduction of iron construction and the rectangular stern windows were gradually phased out in favour of circular ports. Stern carvings such as ropework, badges and stars continued on the better-quality ships like the *Cutty Sark,* which had gilded flowers against a blue background on each quarter linked with gilded cable-laid rope carving with the ship's name and port above it. There was a central star supported by C-shaped carving with the owner's badge below it.

Iron or steel sailing ships tended to have more

austere decoration than their immediate predecessors. Some owners such as T & J Brocklebank, who ran a prestigious cargo service to Bombay, were prepared to pay extra for high-quality carving. Their iron ship *Majestic* of 1875 had a figurehead of Queen Victoria, although there was a hint of frugality because she was painted all white and the fine tendrils in her trailboards were painted and not carved. She also retained a little reminder of the older bow, as between the trailboard and the head rail there were three sloping painted rectangles which represented the vertical head timbers of the beakhead. Many later ships had a figurehead without trailboards and these carvings were often down to a price. In 1890, John Roberts of Glasgow sold one of his stock female figureheads for the four-masted barque *Port Stanley* for only £3 15s. The figurehead of the *Falkirk* of 1896 looked as if she was carved for a low price, having a drain pipe for a neck and the folds

in her clothing were crudely indicated by broad gouge marks. The other cheaper alternative to a figure was a billethead or a coat of arms. The four-masted barque *Archibald Russell* of 1905 was one of the very last sailing ships built. She had a billet head and a shield and yet retained the old-fashioned and expensive painted decoration of dummy gunports. A few shipowners went in for a corporate approach with each ship carrying the same device. The most memorable was the Corsar & Co's Flying Horse Line which all carried a Pegasus on their bow. After the commercial sailing ship had become extinct, a small number of deep-sea square riggers were built for training sailors and most of them have continued the figurehead tradition, though often re-interpreted in a more modern way. The female figurehead of the *Christian Radich* of 1937, for example, was true to the time of her building because her figurehead has an Art Deco look and her trailboards are cut out of steel and riveted to the hull.

Bow of the training ship *Christian Radich* 1937. (J & C McCutcheon Collection)

CHAPTER

Coastal, Inland and Fishing Craft

Before there were railways and decently-paved roads and long before motor vehicles, the cheapest way to move goods in any quantity was by water. This could be along the coast, up estuaries, rivers or man-made canals. The vessels involved were invariably small – about an average of twenty tons in the early seventeenth century – partly because of the size of the cargoes on offer and partly the need to navigate in shallow undredged waters. Inland and coastal trade employed hundreds of vessels all over Europe. Around the British Isles alone the traffic was

immense: by the early nineteenth century, goods were being delivered to and from London by boats from 500 ports, quays or depots. Some of these trades were of long standing. From at least the mid-seventeenth century the cheesemongers of London sent ships up to the Dee or the Mersey estuaries to collect consignments of Cheshire cheese, which was in great demand in the capital. It was cheaper to sail round Land's End than to send the cheese to London by road.

Navigable rivers had been used since as far back

The stern of the schooner *Kathleen and May* 1901.

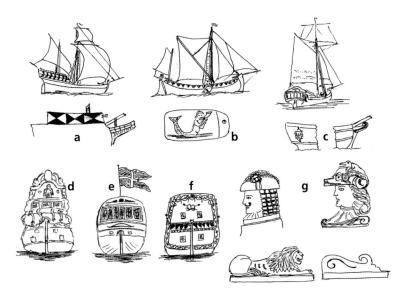

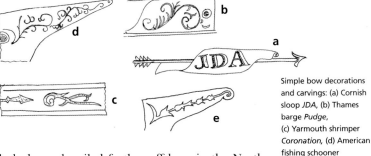

Simple bow decorations and carvings: (a) Cornish sloop *JDA*, (b) Thames barge *Pudge*, (c) Yarmouth shrimper *Coronation*, (d) American fishing schooner *Fredonia*, and (e) ketch *Maude*.

Painted decorations: (a) bow of Maltese dghaisa, (b) wind vane from Norfolk wherry *Jenny Morgan*, (c) Norfolk wherry mast symbols, (d) Norfolk wherry *Zulu's* nameboard, (e) Tyne wherry *Elswick 2*, (f) Honfleur shrimper, and (g) River Elbe jolle.

Seventeenth and eighteenth century coasters: (a) ketch and painted decoration on the *Godspeed* 1607, (b) model of a Dutch smak 1676 with painted leeboards (c) English hoy of 1741 from the Buck Brothers' view of Colchester and the bow and stern of a model of 1750, (d) stern of an English collier bark about 1700, (e) stern of a Danish brig from Koefoed's dictionary 1783, (f) stern of a genoese pinque from Baugean 1814, and (g) four rudderheads: moustachioed gent from Dutch smak 1676, warrior lady and lion from Friesland kof barges and scroll design from galliot *Petronella* 1897.

as Roman times. From the late seventeenth century many were improved by dredging, by straightening out bends and by building locks. They were supplemented by new artificial canals, and by 1800, there was an international network of navigable rivers and canals in Europe. In England they linked booming new industries with ports to export their produce and to import raw materials. By the early nineteenth century, the major waterways had developed their own types of barges. These included keels on the Humber estuary and Yorkshire rivers, trows in the Bristol Channel and the Severn, wherries on the Norfolk Broads and flats on the Mersey. Many different types of inland barge could found all over in Europe and the America as well. The Dutch, whose whole economy was built around water transport and fishing, had a wide variety of galliots, kofs, klippers and others for specific trades or locations.

Fishing was carried on in coastal waters by a wide variety of different types of open boats. Larger,

decked vessels sailed further offshore in the North Sea or even further afield to Iceland or Newfoundland for the rich cod fisheries. Fishing continued under sail right into the twentieth century. As with the inland craft there was a wide variety of different types based in particular localities with a wonderful assortment of names from English bawleys and nobbies, to Scottish scaffies and zulus, French dundees and sinagos, and Dutch hoogars and schokkers.

All these different types of vessel carried much less decoration than their bigger sisters, though most had some, however simple. There were a number of pictorial sources for seventeenth- and

eighteenth-century coasters and fishing boats. The Dutch School of marine painters often depicted smaller vessels as part of a larger seascape, particularly in the foreground, and there were plenty of paintings and photographs of coasters from the mid-nineteenth century onwards. They have been recorded in great detail by twentieth-century maritime historians with whole books devoted to a particular type of vessel. Contemporary models were rare before 1850, but there have been a number of convincing modern reconstructions. There is also a large number of nineteenth and early twentieth century vessels that have been restored and kept sailing. On the technical side, most of these vessels were constructed of wood, and in the early seventeenth century, most were propelled by square sails but by 1700 fore-and-aft rigs were increasingly common. The lateen sail remained the common Mediterranean rig. The schooner rig was the most important development and from the early nineteenth century its combination of sails made for versatile vessels capable of working in coasting and ocean trades. By the late nineteenth century, American shipbuilders were launching huge wooden coastal schooners with up to six masts.

In the seventeenth century, the main type of decoration seems to have been painted designs. An early seventeenth-century ketch had a band of chevrons around its poop, and the modern replica of the little coaster *Godspeed* which crossed the Atlantic in 1607 has triangles of red and white on her upperworks. Although no one can be sure of the exact colour scheme of the *Godspeed*, this simple painted geometric pattern was certainly typical for

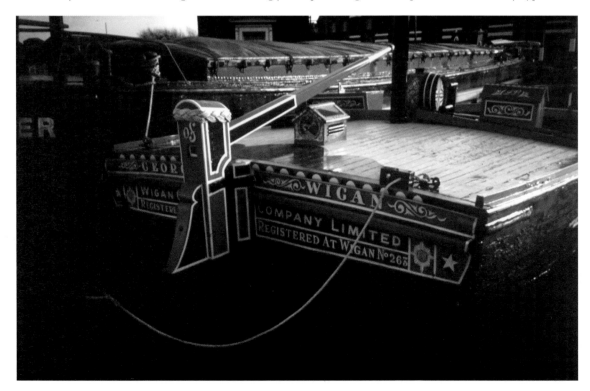

Leeds and Liverpool Canal short boat *George*. (National Waterways Museum, Ellesmere Port)

Left: Portuguese River Tagus fregata.

Middle: Carved tillers at the North Devon Maritime Museum, Appledore.

Right: The figurehead of the Canadian-built schooner *Beatrice*. (National Museums Liverpool)

the time. A model of a Dutch smak dated 1676 in the Rijksmuseum, Amsterdam, has a bold double line of painted triangles along the gunwale and the leeboards painted with a picture of a merman blowing a conch shell. It is not clear whether this was a common decoration, but if it was, then it shows how far Baroque motifs had spread in the maritime world because this was no more than a working boat. Most Dutch small craft seem to have had a decorated rudder head. Their rudder posts were extended upwards above the top of the stern and were finished off with a carved head. The tiller also might be brightly painted in geometric patterns such as diamonds or triangles, and a carving on top of the rudder head remained a feature in the eighteenth and on into the late nineteenth century. The 1676 smak had a moustachioed, bewigged man. Two late eighteenth-century heads from Friesland barges known as kofs were a lion and a woman in a Classical helmet, carved in the shape of a dolphin's head with a crest in the shape of a crocodile. There is a similar

Amazon rudder head figure in the Norwegian Maritime Museum, Oslo, and these both demonstrate how Classical influences could spread down as far as humble sailing barges. Later rudder head carvings were simplified, however. For example, the steel galliot *Petronella* built at Groningen in 1897 only had a simple scroll.

The eighteenth-century English hoys conveyed passengers and 'general cargoes' in small consignments and ran regular services from outlying places to major ports, often running to a timetable. Shopkeepers and the local gentry relied on them to deliver goods ordered from London. In return, hoys could deliver consignments of foodstuffs such as barley for brewing beer, cheese or cured fish. The Buck brothers' engravings of Colchester and Ipswich show hoys as single-masted and similar in outline to the Royal Yacht *Mary* with carved ornament around their stern windows. A model of a hoy dated about 1750 in the National Maritime Museum had a fiddlehead and single windows on each quarter with carving round them.

The gammon knee of the *Bessie Clark*. (Mark Myers)

For many coasters the stern rather than the bow tended to be the main area for decoration. Larger coasters such as a Whitby collier of around 1700, or a Danish brig illustrated by Koefoed in 1783 or a Genoese pinque engraved by Baugean in the early 1800s, had carvings that were much the same as contemporary deep-sea ships. The collier, whose descent from the fluit was clear, had a shield and a figure in the taffrail area with decorated S-shaped brackets below the stern windows. The Danish brig's stern was dominated by the stern windows. There was a small shield supported by foliage and a section of carved ropework below to contain the ship's name. The pinque was more ornamental with a chain of S-shaped foliage running right around the edges of the stern with a band of triangles separating the upper and lower decks. There was also a badge of war trophies in the centre of the upper stern. It was not unlike the carved stern of the baghla dhow. Simple carvings picked out in contrasting colours at the stern were common. A popular form was a semi-circle of carved rope picked out in yellow to highlight the ship's name and port. The schooner *Kathleen and May* of 1901, which is still sailing, has this kind of device. Scandinavian coasters often had a carved star at either side of their flat transom stern possibly with their name and port carved on decorative panels.

Carved nameboards might also be fitted on the bows. There are some good examples such as that from the *Jernaes* in the Sunderland Volunteer Lifesaving Association's Watchhouse. Carved and painted nameboards were also seen on British coasters and fishing boats. That of the early nineteenth-century Cornish sloop *JDA*, which is in the Padstow Museum, is a white arrow with a blue

The bow of the *Kathleen and May*.

Mid-Victorian figurehead on a house on the Lleyn Peninsula.

1950s. Such was the strength of tradition, and this has continued with the restored barges of today. The *Pudge*'s present bow-boards were carved only in the last few years. *Topsail*, the Journal of the Society for Sailing Barge Research, has recorded many other examples. You can also see them on the twenty or so barges that are still kept sailing. The jolles, which were the sailing barge on the lower Elbe in Germany, had a painted variation with two bunches of tulips painted on either side of the hawseholes for the anchor cables.

Another common combination was carved or painted names at the bow and an incised line picked out in yellow or white running back to the stern. The Tyne wherry *Elswick 2* of 1913 at Beamish Museum had her name carved in block letters with simple leaf work all in white on either side and a broad red line below. The shrimper *Coronation* of 1902 at the Time and Tide Museum, Great Yarmouth, had another variation. She did not have a carved name but a simple carved scroll picked out in yellow against a blue top plank. Behind it there was an incised line starting with an arrowhead which ran all the way to the stern. Some of the American East Coast fishing schooners had a more complex version of the *Coronation*'s ornament, which was painted in white on the bow and ran back to the hawseholes. The illustrated example is from a photograph of the schooner *Fredonia* in 1889. There were also much plainer paint schemes on fishing boats, which relied on a combination of colours such as red waterline, white hull and blue topsides. This kind of combination could be seen anywhere from lateen-rigged Turkish fishing caiques to Cromer crab boats. The shrimpers fishing from the French port of Honfleur, for example, were painted black with a yellow line along their topsides and a large white triangle on their bows.

scroll wrapped about its centre with the name carved across it. Thames sailing barges, which developed into coasters in the nineteenth century, had bow and quarter boards which were carved with incised patterns derived from the acanthus leaf motif. There are many variations and the carved lines were usually painted yellow with a green background. The name and port might be carved directly into or painted on to the barge's stern, a tradition that continued right until the end of wooden barge building. For example the *Pudge,* which was built in 1922, was fitted with these badges and continued to display them even when she was cut down to a motor barge in the

While painting was a quicker and cheaper way to decorate small vessels than carving, some paint schemes were highly complex. Norfolk wherries, for example, had black hulls with a white patch on the bow and on deck there was plenty of red, white and blue. The front of the hold carried decorative boards with the name and the owner. Those from the wherry *Zulu* at the Time and Tide Museum had a red scroll with yellow lettering on a black background. The painter must have been inexperienced because the D in Catfield has slipped off the end of the scroll. The tops of the wherries' masts were painted in various combinations according to the owner and carried a device such as a star or a swastika-like emblem. The Leeds and Liverpool Canal's short boat was another good British example. The restored short boat *George* is preserved at the Ellesmere Port Boat Museum and her stern and the top of her rudder were divided into a series of red and blue panels which were outlined in white. Apart from her name, port and owners, there were motifs such as stars, triangles in alternating colours and scrolls. The deck fittings such as the water barrel and the cabin skylight were given the same treatment. The most extreme British form of painted decoration was on narrow canal boats. Their style is a complex topic, which has been dealt with in A J Lewery's *Flowers Afloat*. Highly-painted boats were found in other parts of Europe. The Portuguese fishing boats and barges had distinctive designs. A Tagus sailing barge, a fregata, had a yellow and white hull with the rubbing strakes in black. The gunwale was white and blue with a yellow panel on which were painted a trail of red roses. There were more roses below and on the top of the stem. The ferry boats in Valletta harbour in Malta – the dghaisas – had topsides with a series of C-shaped leafy scrolls, two hull colours such white below the waterline and red above and a carved and

Three figureheads at the Sunderland Lifesaving Association. (A J Lewery)

painted back rest for the passengers' seat.

Like the dghaisa's backrest, coasters could have one or two small pieces of carving. Some of the late nineteenth century canal narrow-boats had their names carved in the top plank at the stern, while some coastal schooners had deck fittings such as skylights with carving on them. Carved tillers were a popular feature especially on fishing boats, where they might have a spiral down in the centre of the shaft and a carved boss on the end. There are three good examples in the North Devon Maritime Museum; the one in the centre from the *Village Girl* has finely carved accurate decorative ropework. The larger ones might also have the name of the vessel carved in the sides like that from the trawler *Driver* in the Docklands Museum, London. The wind vane or bob could add a distinctive touch to many sailing craft. This consisted of a figure or symbol cut out or pierced in sheet metal with a long trailing pennant. Norfolk wherries, for example, often had figures reflecting their names, like the wherry *Jenny Morgan*

Classical figurehead on the schooner *Volant*. (V C Boyle Archive, North Devon Maritime Museum)

which had a woman in a Welsh hat. The *Harriet*, a salt barge on the Severn, had her name painted on the vane with a bottle and glass cut out of brass above it. The crews of these small craft could be very proud of their wind vanes. The late Dick Hart of Widnes recalled how as a lad before 1914 he had climbed the mast of a rival, the *Pilgrim*, and pinched her gleaming brass cockerel to put on his own ship, the *Ceres*, and the serious row that ensued. These were all small and simply-designed but they added a touch of distinctiveness to a ship, something which their crews could take pride in.

There are a large number of figureheads that survive from coasting vessels, partly because many coasters were wrecked on the shore rather than far out at sea, and their figureheads could be more easily salvaged. A second reason was that their carvings were much smaller than those of their deep-sea sisters, and so were far more likely to be preserved by private individuals. The Canadian-built schooner *Beatrice* ended up as a sand barge at Widnes in the 1930s and when she was broken up Jim Pennington, the man who ran the local steam dredger, cut off her figurehead and took her home. Another reason was that sailing coasters survived as commercial carriers in much greater numbers into the twentieth century. However, there were many coastal vessels that did not carry figureheads. For example, the Shipping Register at Wells in North Norfolk recorded 112 new ships between 1832 and 1845, only two of these having figureheads, the new schooners *Caroline* and *Little Helen* which both had

Left: The figurehead of the schooner *Jane Slade* 1875. (Helen Doe)

Far left: The badge carving of the ketch *Emma Louise* 1883. (North Devon Maritime Museum)

female busts. I get the impression that figureheads were less common among the East Coast ports than in the West Coast ones. It may be of course that sail lasted longer in the West.

The most basic figurehead was a decorated gammon knee, which could be either carved or painted. The one from the ketch *Bessie Clark* built at Bideford in 1881 had a seagull carved by a series of shallow lines which were emphasised with white paint. Carved scrolling foliage was more usual. The *Maude*'s simple thistle design was recorded at Appledore in 1947. The last surviving schooner, the *Kathleen and May*, has a much more extended carving, starting with a small boss and stretching

back with a tendril of acanthus with shamrocks and roses. Another form was a billet head with or without a shield. That of the *Emma Louise* of 1883, also in the North Devon Maritime Museum, had this arrangement with a Union Jack painted on the shield enclosed in a C-shaped scroll – a conceit going back to the Baroque era. American coasters were usually had a billet head and carved trailboards, and good examples of these can be found in J S Hanna's book on maritime carving.

Most of the coasters' figureheads were of human beings and the majority of those were female, being perhaps members of the owner's family or business associates. Some of the late nineteenth-century

Portmadoc schooners had un-Welsh names such as *Frau Minna Petersen* of 1891 or *Anna Braunschweig* of 1876 after wives or daughters of business associates in Hamburg who took many cargoes of Welsh roofing slates. The Cornish schooner *Jane Slade* of 1870 had a portrait bust of the remarkable Jane Slade who, on the death of her husband in 1870, took over and ran his shipbuilding, shipowning, property and public house business in Polruan. Her figurehead still survives in this little Cornish town and it can be readily seen that has been carved from life. This was a well-carved piece, especially her face, though the recent restoration of the paintwork makes her look rather like Joan Collins! Many of the survivors cannot been identified, although some of the females can be dated by their dress. Of the trio at the Sunderland Volunteer Lifesaving Association, one in the centre is in Highland dress with a bonnet and a sash, while the other two with their bustles probably dated from the late 1870s or early 1880s. Some females were carved in Classical dress, the maiden on the schooner *Volant* built at Kirkwall in 1877 being a good example. Many also carried a bunch of flowers clutched to their chests, a traditional symbol of purity and maidenhood, and roses were particularly associated with the Virgin Mary. Whether the ship carvers were aware of these connotations or whether they simply inherited the motif is impossible to determine.

There were male figureheads as well. Naval and military heroes were to be found along with more stolid portraits of owners such as that found on the side of a house on the Lleyn peninsula in North Wales. There were also more unusual carvings such as that of the Runcorn schooner *Harvest King* of 1879 in Arklow Maritime Museum, whose figurehead sported the beard of an Old Testament prophet and clutched a sickle and a sheaf of corn. There was also the occasional animal or bird. The

schooner *Bee*, built at Barnstaple in 1846, which had a figurehead of a bee hive rather than a bee, was unusual, and presumably the Sunderland ship called *Home Brewed Beer* must have had a foaming tankard or a barrel, or possibly a John Bull figure with a pint pot similar to the one drawn by R Lee.

Figurehead of the schooner *Harvest King*. (Arklow Maritime Museum)

Steamers and Motor Vessels

The early nineteenth century ushered in an era of massive expansion in industrial production and world trade, coupled with unprecedented technological progress. By the end of the century, the sailing ship had been relegated to a subsidiary role in bulk trades, coasting and fishing. The twentieth century saw technology advance ever faster. Marred as it was by two World Wars, nonetheless these conflicts accelerated the development new maritime technologies such as welded construction, diesel engines and electronics. It seemed unlikely that something as traditional and functionally useless as a figurehead should continue to have a place in this environment. Yet somehow it did, although in a very small way. Sources of information for steam ships'

decoration are numerous. Apart from the obvious secondary sources of paintings and models, the invention of photography in the 1840s provided precise documentation for many figureheads. There are also a number of preserved steamers, both warships and merchant ships, and quite a few figureheads and other carvings.

The first experimental steamers dated back to the 1780s, but steamships did not become viable commercial vessels until the 1820s. At first they were propelled by paddles, then screw propellers were

Chilean destroyer *Captain O'Brien* with bow badge, 1901.

tried in the 1830s and became the norm by the 1860s. Economical compound engines developed from the late 1850s, and they made it possible for steam ships to compete with sailing ships on profitable long-distance routes. Iron hulls of the largest size were launched from the 1840s. By the early twentieth century the steam turbine had become a practical propulsion system and oil fuel had been introduced. Diesel engines gradually took over from steam engines and ships with welded steel hulls grew bigger and bigger. From the 1880s new types of merchant ships such as tankers were developed. Since 1945, there have been revolutionary changes in cargo-carrying with the introduction of new kinds of ships, container ships and roll-on roll-off ferries being particular examples. The first twenty years of the twentieth century also saw the development of the submarine and the aircraft carrier – warships of the greatest strategic importance.

All the early steam ships followed the form of sailing ships. Many of them had figureheads, stern carvings and quarter galleries, and sails were also carried to assist the engines up until the 1880s, although sails on warships became increasingly incompatible with the need for a stable gun platform and a clear field of fire for the new gun turrets. By about 1870 most large steamers, except for those

The sloop HMS *Gannet* 1878 in dock at Chatham. (Chatham Historic Dockyard Trust)

owned by a few particular companies, were built with straight stems. At the same time the ram bow – the reverse of a clipper bow's shape – became an important feature of warship design. Neither of these changes necessarily led to the discarding of bow decoration, but it became increasingly perfunctory

and reduced to no more than a badge or a small plaque of carved foliage. It was the same for stern decorations.

In the 1850s, the majority of battleships were still wooden vessels with broadsides of muzzle-loading guns firing broadsides (though many had been equipped with auxiliary steam engines) and they also had figureheads. However, naval restrictions on expenditure for figureheads continued, and most were usually busts, or demi-figureheads. There were also warships built of iron and fitted with paddles and armed as gunboats or frigates from the 1840s which also had figureheads. HMS *Virago* was a 1,059-ton wooden paddle sloop of 1842 and her figurehead is preserved at Chatham Historic Dockyard. It was carved by one of the Hellyer family and is small for the size of ship. She

The eagle of the steam frigate USS *Lancaster* 1875. (The Mariners' Museum, Newport News)

is depicted in eighteenth-century dress with one breast exposed and carrying a flaming torch, intended to symbolize the older meaning of virago as a bold, courageous woman. Her hand carrying the torch appears to be too big for the rest of her body. Paddle warships were unsatisfactory in battle because the paddles were vulnerable to enemy fire and after the 1840s all fighting warships were screw propelled. The most important advance was the building of the armoured iron 'frigate' HMS *Warrior* of 1860. She was the most powerful ship of her day and her figurehead, which has been re-created for her restoration, was a splendid Classical warrior brandishing a sword and a shield. The Devonport Dockyard collection includes another fine figurehead from a near sister-ship HMS *Resistance*. Carved by Cornelius Luck of London for only £22 18s, bare-chested in a toga he is the epitome of resistance, his muscles, hair and facial expression of indomitable fierceness being executed with accuracy and subtlety. He is currently on show at the Scottish Maritime Museum, Irvine. Luck also carved the original gannet figurehead for the sloop HMS *Gannet* of 1878. This Victorian 'gunboat' is preserved at the Chatham Historic Dockyard and was built as a patrol boat capable of keeping the peace in remote

colonies. She had a full set of sails as well as engines to extend her cruising range. Her gannet was typical of the figureheads of the smaller Victorian warships. They tended to be given more prosaic names. HMS *Wasp, Hornet, Cracker* or *Plumper* were names of some of the steam sloops laid down in 1847, and *Gnat, Dwarf, Flirt* and *Growler* were from the *Beacon* class of 1867.

The United States Navy had fitted billet heads to most of its nineteenth-century ships, but the steam frigate USS *Lancaster* of 1875 was a glorious exception. This splendid gilded eagle was fitted on a ram bow. Its carver, J H Bellamy, had carved every one of its feathers on its outstretched wings. The photograph on page 79 was taken at the Mariner's Museum, Newport News, Virginia on the occasion of a *Titanic* commemorative dinner. The eagle was dressed appropriately for this banquet. Other European navies followed a similar technical progression as that of the Royal Navy. While hulls were built of iron and steam engines were fitted, the old wood and sail navies' traditions in decoration lingered on. The quality of their figureheads tended to be higher than those of the Royal Navy. That of the Swedish steam corvette *Saga* of 1879 (see page 82) followed the standard set by Törnström at the start of the nineteenth century, being both anatomically correct and dramatic in its gesture. In 1887, the last figurehead to be carved for the Royal Navy was a crude portrait of the great naval hero for the battleship HMS *Rodney* of 1887, which did him no justice (see page 82). Fortunately he, along with all other naval figureheads, was ordered to be removed in 1897. The royal coat of arms mounted on a shield carved with Baroque detail and supported by gilded foliage, and mounted either on the bow or the stern, was a common type of carving for iron warships. There is a fine example on the huge model of HMS *Northumberland* of 1866 in the Docklands Museum in London. Even in the early twentieth century, there was often some residual decoration around the bows. The destroyer *Capitan O'Brien* of 1901 which was built for the Chilean Navy by Lairds of Birkenhead in 1901 had a bow decoration. It is likely that these later decorations were cast in brass or cast iron from wooden patterns. The exceptions were a small number of sail training ships which continued to be built for some navies such as those of Argentina, Chile, Germany, France, Spain, Italy and Sweden

Great Britain led the world in the development of iron merchant steamers, and by the second half of the nineteenth century the shipyards of the Clyde and Tyne and Wear were supplying a considerable proportion of the new steamers launched. This is why all the examples cited below are British-built. By the late 1830s, there had been sufficient technical progress to enable large paddle steamers to steam the 3,000 miles from Europe to North America. These paddle liners were prestige vessels. The figurehead of the 703-ton wooden paddle steamer *Sirius* which made two voyages from London to New York in 1838 has survived. This was a realistic carving of a leaping rough-coated spaniel, intended to symbolize Sirius, the Dog Star. Given its position and the delicacy of its limbs, it is a wonder it survived

The dog figurehead from the paddle steamer *Sirius* 1837. (Hull Maritime Museum)

the Atlantic storms. It is now one of the star exhibits in Hull Maritime Museum's collection. The Cunard Line started a mail and passenger service across the Atlantic in 1840, employing large paddle steamers that were beautifully decorated, which was probably more than a matter of pride. They intended to make their ships more elegant than their rivals in their efforts to attract passengers to this new form of travel. In the early 1850s the ships of their main rival, the American Collins Line, had straight bows and a functional appearance. Cunard emphasised tradition, and by extension safety and reliability. Their *Persia* of 1856 was among the most beautiful steamers ever built. Her clipper bow was graced with a female in flowing robes representing the Roman province of Persia (all Cunard ships were named after Roman Imperial provinces). Her paddle boxes had C-shaped scrolls around a central carving which contained other traditional features such as crossed swords. Her stern carvings would have fitted equally well on a sailing ship. The decoration of the paddle boxes was continued on later paddle steamers with straight stems. This was usually a semi-circular

badge on the straight section close to the waterline with slots radiating out from it rather like the rays of the sun. The badge might have been a symbol such as a star or the company's coat of arms, but it could also be something more realistic such as the cameo of Queen Victoria from the Thames estuary excursion steamer *Royal Sovereign* of 1893. This is part of the excellent paddle-steamer display at Felixstowe Museum.

The screw-propelled iron steamer *Great Britain* of 1843 was a technological pioneer but conservative in her hull decoration. Her restoration at Bristol has put this back in its original design with painted ports and a crowned royal coat of arms supported by a lion and

unicorn carved in relief. The design of the trailboard was curious, with gilded symbols of Victorian trade, industry, learning, art and agriculture dotted along its sixteen-foot length. To starboard, there is a sheaf of corn, a globe, a lyre and trumpets, an artist's pallet, a book and a bunch of flowers. To port (as you can see in the illustration) there was a coil of rope, two gear wheels, a dove of peace, a carpenter's square and a medical staff (a caduceus). At her stern, there were false quarter galleries with swans and cornucopia, and the stern itself also recalled a bygone age with two unicorns supporting the coat of arms of Bristol.

Owners and their marine superintendants of this era had all grown up with sail, and so it is

Queen Victoria on the paddle box of the *Royal Sovereign* 1893. (Felixstowe Museum)

perhaps not surprising that some of its traditions such as carvings at the bow and stern were perpetuated. Clipper bows and figureheads started to disappear from new ships in the 1870s. Cunard, for example, ordered their first two straight-stemmed liners in 1870, and in the same year P&O who dominated the mail and passenger services to India, China and Australia ordered their last ship with a figurehead. However, some liner companies chose to retain the older shape and a figurehead even though the less complex straight stem was cheaper to build. The Inman Line founded in 1851 opted to retain the older shape of bow and decorated stern right down to the last ship they had built – the *City of Rome* of 1881. It was a trademark, along with their black funnels with a single white stripe. The faded photograph of their *City of New York* of 1865 shows the new figurehead fitted in 1886 after a collision. Like its predecessor and all the other Inman ships, the city was symbolized by a mature woman in a flowing gown with a double line of florid foliage trailing behind her. The upper one

carried the name and a small badge of the Stars and the Stripes. The Inman Line was not unique. Other shipping companies lines ordered ships with clipper bows and figureheads. Perhaps the main reasons were ones of tradition and pride, and from a

The port bow of the *Great Britain* 1843.

commercial point of view they did make their ships stand out from the rest. This was precisely what the National Line did in 1884 with their new liner *America*. All their previous ships had had straight stems. By the 1880s, they were suffering from the intense competition for carrying passengers across the Atlantic. As a final bid, they ordered the 5,528-ton *America*. She was intended to be the fastest and most beautiful ship on the Atlantic, and she too was built with a clipper bow, but unfortunately one beautiful ship was not enough to save the line. After years of running sailing ships to New Zealand, Shaw Savill and Albion ordered their first steamer, the *Arawa* in 1884. They kept the sailing ship traditions with painted ports, lots of sails, a clipper bow and a figurehead. By 1905 the *Arawa* had been sold to the grandly-titled Imperial Direct West India Mail

Service Company. This had been set up not only to carry cargo (especially bananas) but also to develop the tourist traffic to Jamaica. Sea cruises were beginning to be popular with the wealthy and were often recommended for convalescents or sufferers of tuberculosis. So, the *Arawa*, which had already been renamed once as the *Lake Megantic*, became the new white painted, yacht-like *Port Henderson*.

Some cargo steamer companies also persisted with figureheads. Two Scottish shipowners, the Aberdeen Line and the Ben Line of Leith, were two examples of sailing ship firms changing over to steamers in order to continue their services. They were managed by the families who founded them, and there was a great sense of pride and desire to be distinctive even though this might add to the building costs. The Aberdeen Line's ships were

Figurehead of the Inman liner *City of New York* 1865. (The Thomas Family)

named after heroes of Ancient Greece with figureheads to match, and their hulls were painted in a special shade of green which made them stand out at a time when most ships' hulls were painted black. The Ben Line bought their first steamers in 1881 when their service to China and Japan was advertised as the Clipper Line of Steamers. This certainly set them apart from their competitors. They had another nineteen ships built with clipper bows and female figureheads up to 1914 and their much-admired appearance inspired the nickname 'the Leith yachts'. The Prince Line of Newcastle was started in 1884 by James Knott, a local shipbroker who dabbled in owning sailing ships. His new steamer company was intended to run freight services from Newcastle to the Mediterranean had a fleet of new steamers built between 1884 and 1893.

All had 'Prince' names with the Prince of Wales' feathers on the funnel, and all had an individually carved figurehead which reflected their name. That of the *Carib Prince* built in 1893 was carved by David Hughes of Liverpool, and depicted the chieftain one of the tribes of indigenous peoples of Central America in a feathered headdress and skirt clutching a curved dagger. The short trailboards also carried the feathers of the Prince of Wales. This figurehead represented the typical late nineteenth-century steamer figurehead, which were almost all three-quarter-length carvings of human beings. It is difficult to quantify, but I have the impression that were more female figureheads than male ones. One exception can be seen at the Manchester Science Museum. The model of the *Salfordia* of 1898, which was the first ship of the Manchester and Salford

Prince Line's *Carib Prince* 1893. (The Thomas Family)

Steam Ship Co, carried the coat of arms of the city. She reflected both the civic pride engendered by the opening of the Manchester Ship Canal four years earlier and the need to build up its cargo traffic.

There were also smaller ships built with figureheads. The whalers which were owned in some numbers at Dundee, Hull and Peterhead in the latter part of the nineteenth century were stoutly built wooden steamers, which were usually barque rigged. The Antarctic research ships, such as the *Discovery* of 1901 which is preserved at Dundee, were based on their design. Most carried a simple billet head and trailboards with a piece of carved ropework on the stern. There were also a number of coastal steamers with figureheads, which were not paddle steamers. They were all ships on regular routes carrying passengers as well as cargo. The *Kintyre* of 1868 ran regular services between Glasgow and Campbeltown until she was sunk in a collision in 1907. Her beautiful appearance inspired a fulsome obituary in the *Campbeltown Courier*: 'Who on the route did not

know her? She was inimitable. Her successors were but sorry imitations of her beauty . . . Forward her beautiful cutwater, curving out to the inimitable bowsprit, put her in a class alone, and all her lines were in a beauteous symmetry'. This might seem far-fetched but steamers, especially ones with figureheads, could attract that sort of praise, and so it made economic sense for some owners to beautify

Right: Figurehead of the Scottish coastal steamer *Claymore* 1881. (Scottish Maritime Museum)

Below: New bulk carrier *John Oldendorff* with painted badge and 'trailboards'.

their ships with figureheads. The Scottish coastal steamer *Claymore* of 1881 sailed on similar services around the Hebrides. She had a striking carving of a Highlander wielding a claymore sword and painted in white with gilded details. The *Claymore* and similar vessels attracted passengers who wished to enjoy the spectacular scenery of northern Scotland. Even as late as 1930, the North of Scotland and Orkney and Shetland Steam Navigation Company ordered a clipper-bowed steamer, the *St Sunniva*, for carrying passengers on cruises. Other companies used the same ploy; for example, the motor ship *Stella Polaris* was built in Sweden in 1927 for Clipper AB for cruising had a clipper bow and a figurehead. The other later type of steamers with figureheads were the yachts of the wealthy. They were fashionable and they provided a mobile hotel to cruise the world. Just as with the *Kintyre*, a yacht with a clipper bow and a figurehead was considered beautiful, distinctive and likely to impress your friends. The

figurehead of the 910-ton steam yacht *Miranda II* built for Lord Leith in 1909 was a carving of a young woman painted white with a gilded necklace and sash. She must have been intended to portray the heroine of Shakespeare's play, *The Tempest*. In the First World War she was requisitioned as a convoy escort vessel and was then bought by Trinity House as an inspection vessel. In the 1950s, her figurehead finally ended up outside the Trinity house maintenance depot at Great Yarmouth, and I do not know whether she was saved when the depot closed.

A late and unusual piece of carving was fitted on the sterns of all the Isle of Man Steam Packet ships built in the 1940s and 1950s. The one from the *King*

Orry of 1946 has been preserved at the Museum of Liverpool Life. This carving was circular with ropework round its edge and the Legs of Man, the badge of the island, in the centre. The company goes back to 1830 and its paddle steamers had the same carving on their paddle boxes and even the company's modern ships have the Legs of Man badge painted on their bows. Bow carvings or painted scrolls around the hawseholes were to be found on a surprising number of smaller ships such as tugs. Some wooden steam fishing boats were given bow badges with their names carved into them. There is a collection of these at the Lowestoft Maritime Museum. The bow decoration has been continued in some later fishing vessels but only in paint. The trawler *Caroline Elizabeth*, which was based at Newlyn in 1994, is a good example, with three bold white stripes and stars and red scrollwork. She was owned by a local family, the Stevensons, who took great pride not only in their appearance of their ships but also in that of their refrigerated delivery lorries, which had pictures of the Stevenson

Isle of Man stern badge from the *King Orry* 1946. (National Museums Liverpool)

trawlers painted on their sides.

The raked bow with its rounded top section was introduced in the 1930s, and it provided a space for a badge or an emblem. Cargo liner companies such as the Elder Dempster and the Shaw Savill lines had metal coats of arms, while others had simpler painted badges which were often the initial letters of the company's name. They were accompanied by two or three painted stripes on either side, which were the ghost of a trailboard and which can still be seen on some modern ships. The Olsen Line of Norway was the only company to continue the figurehead tradition after the Second World War. They commissioned figureheads for their new vessels and some of these were made of different materials such as bronze and glass mosaic. Today, ships continue to have a form of hull decoration in paint. The funnel is often the main focus and can carry the company colours and logo, while ferry and cruise liner companies have sometimes gone in for bold overall paint designs which feature their names or logos or even their website addresses. Painted bow badges can still be spotted: for example, the 31,000-ton bulk carrier *John Oldendorff* which was only built in 2002 carries two red 'trailboard' stripes and the badge of her managers, Seafarer's Shipping Inc. of Manila.

Carving on ships could be inside the ship as well as outside. By the late nineteenth century passenger lines competed for first-class passengers by offering a kind of floating version of the grand hotels of Europe. Whereas early liners had relatively plain public spaces, the reconstructed dining saloon on the *Great Britain* being a good example, later liners such as the White Star Lines' *Olympic* and *Titanic* had restaurants, lounges and vast staircases which imitated the carved and gilded interiors of royal palaces. Much of this work would have been carved by the same craftsmen who had worked on

CHAPTER *9*

Carving and Carvers

Previous writers on this subject have implied that ship carving was a rather esoteric craft separated from other kinds of wood carving. In a sense, this might be true of the carvers trained in the various royal dockyards, although even there they would called on to carry out interior work as well as ship work, but ship carving shared the same techniques and often the same designs as other kinds of wood carving and carvers moved from one type of work to another as and when required. The great furniture designer Thomas Sheraton identified four types of wood carving in his *Cabinet Dictionary* of 1803: architectural, internal decoration such as frames for pier glasses, chair work (furniture) and ship work. The latter included 'mass figures for the heads and bold foliage for the sterns and quarters of ships'.

Wood for ship carvings had to be capable of taking a sharp clean cut to ensure that the features were as sharp and clear as possible, as most of the carvings were viewed from a distance. The wood also had to be capable of resisting rot and the harsh maritime environment. No one to my knowledge has done a survey of the species of wood used by taking samples from actual figureheads, but the woods most usually mentioned in the records were oak and pine especially yellow pine. I have also found one reference to elm. In 1825 Overton and Faldo charged £3 for two elm trail boards for the new naval brig HMS *African*, but the account did not state what the figurehead was carved from. Large or complicated figureheads would be made up from several timbers, and some had detachable arms which could be

removed before setting sail. In 1996, the Australian National Maritime Museums X-rayed their eighteenth-century figure of a midshipman holding an octant. Although he stood outside a nautical instrument seller's shop and not on the bow of a ship, he had been carved in the same way as a figurehead. They found he was made up from eight separate pieces. The large figurehead from HMS *Hastings*,

The title page of Laurie and Whittle's pamphlet of 1799.

Carving tools in the
Sheffield Tools Catalogue
1908.

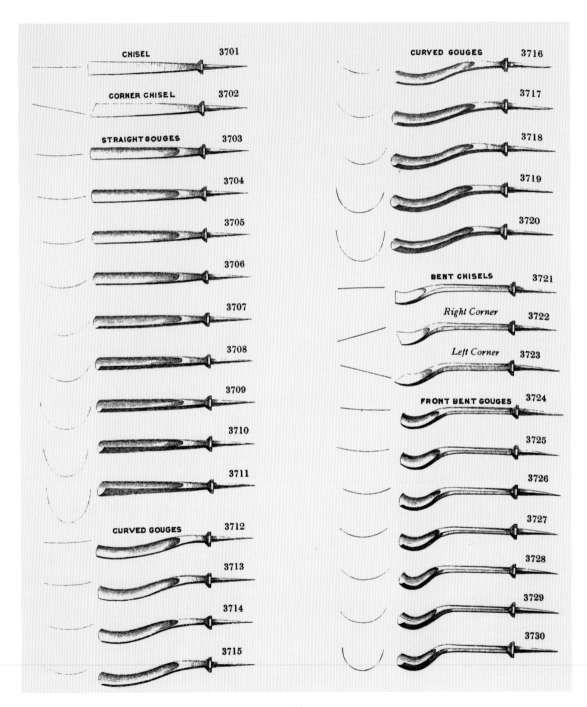

Far left above: Drawing of female figurehead by J J Laurie of Glasgow. (Private Collection)

Far left below: Pencil sketch from William Dodd's notebook. (National Museums Liverpool)

Left: William Dodd's self-portrait bust. (National Museums Liverpool)

which weighs about a ton, was found to be made up of series of vertical slabs dowelled together by copper bolts. The arms were especially vulnerable to damage and needed to have the grain of the wood running down their length to ensure maximum strength.

The procedure for planning the piece varied. The great naval archives contain detailed drawings, the most elaborate being those from the French naval dockyards in the seventeenth and eighteenth centuries. The Danes produced wax models of proposed new figureheads, and there is a fine collection of these in the Danish Naval Museum in Copenhagen. They would have been made to satisfy the controllers of their navy as well as for the guidance of the carver. A shipbuilder needing a new figurehead might send an outline specification along with its name and dimensions to a ship carving firm. The latter would then come forward with proposals for the design and a price for the work. In major shipbuilding centres, shipbuilders might seek prices from several carving firms, although on the other hand some shipbuilders maintained a constant relationship with one firm. Ship carvers kept records of their past work

Right: The late Jack Whitehead and Norman Gaches working on a new figurehead for HMS *Warrior.* The main details have been bosted in.

Far right: A finished figurehead in David Hughes' workshop awaiting painting. Note all the pieces of reference carvings and the tool racks in the background. (The Thomas Family)

for reference. A P Elder's (1828–*c.*1870) note-book, which is in the National Maritime Museum, Greenwich contains fifty-three drawings of figureheads and twelve of stern carvings, all meticulously drawn in Indian ink. By contrast, William Dodd, who was working in Liverpool from the 1850s to about 1921, kept a small notebook of simple pencil sketches, while David Hughes at Liverpool (1847–1923) kept a photographic record of his work. His workshops also contained numerous carvings of ornamental motifs for reference. Some figureheads were modeled from life, David Hughes using his family as models. His daughter posed for the figurehead of the *Kate Thomas* and his wife was frequently used for other sailing ship figureheads, and he even modelled a figurehead of a Chinese mandarin on himself! Figurehead carvers could also

draw inspiration from books and prints. There were general works on shipbuilding such as that of Thomas Sutherland, which had sections on ship carving. There were pattern books covering a wide variety of ornamental designs for carvers such as those published by the ship and furniture carver Thomas Johnson. He began producing prints of Rococo designs as a part-work in 1755 and followed them up with his first major work *A New Book of Ornaments* was published in 1757. While he was aiming his work at furniture carvers, some of his inspirations could be used in ship work around the stern and the supporters of the figurehead. The only publication that I have found that was specifically directed at ship carvers was *A new Book of Ornaments for the use of all who are conversant any way in designing, carving, painting and drawing ships*, first published in 1790 and again in

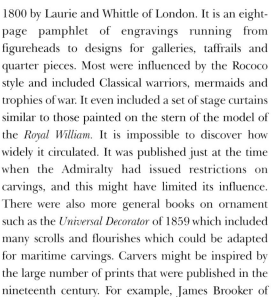

Left: David Hughes as he carved himself as a Chinese mandarin. (The Thomas Family)

Far left: The figurehead for the four-masted barque *Kate Thomas* was modeled by David Hughes' daughter. (The Thomas Family)

1800 by Laurie and Whittle of London. It is an eight-page pamphlet of engravings running from figureheads to designs for galleries, taffrails and quarter pieces. Most were influenced by the Rococo style and included Classical warriors, mermaids and trophies of war. It even included a set of stage curtains similar to those painted on the stern of the model of the *Royal William*. It is impossible to discover how widely it circulated. It was published just at the time when the Admiralty had issued restrictions on carvings, and this might have limited its influence. There were also more general books on ornament such as the *Universal Decorator* of 1859 which included many scrolls and flourishes which could be adapted for maritime carvings. Carvers might be inspired by the large number of prints that were published in the nineteenth century. For example, James Brooker of

Maryport was known to have been inspired by a print of Venus and Adonis when he carved the double figurehead for the ship *Dinapore* in 1851.

There were three main types of carving: carving in relief on a flat block for such components as trail boards, letter-cutting which was counted as a separate technique, and carving in the round for figureheads. The piece of wood to be carved had to be firmly fastened down and an outline of the first cuts drawn on it. This was known as 'blocking in', a roughing-out of the outline of the figure using heavy tools such as a broad axe and a saw to remove large areas of waste wood. The whole process of carving was one of subtraction, of cutting away material to develop the form of the carving. This was followed by 'bosting in', which was the real shaping process. It involved a high level of skill because it was difficult to see the shape and any mistake that took something away could not be amended. The final stage of 'bosting in' involved smoothing-off the piece ready for the last stage which was the carving-in of the small details such as eyes, flowers or jewellery. This involved a technique known as 'chip carving' where angled cuts were made to produce a triangular-shaped depression.

The ship carver needed many hand tools to carry on his craft. The Sheffield Tools Catalogue of 1906 (see page 90) illustrated about sixty different types, and this number could be multiplied by the number of widths of blade. The gouges, which were round-bladed chisels, were most often used, and there were ten basic widths from half an inch to two inches. Some had straight blades, others were spoon-shaped, while some had cranked handles for getting into awkward places. The shallowest were used for smoothing. Then there were V-shaped parting tools for incised lettering and creating textures which generally came with three different angles of forty-five, sixty and ninety degrees. Skew chisels with angled blades were used for cleaning waste wood from corners. Veiners and fluters were U-shaped and macaronis had blades with a flat bottom and vertical sides. All these tools were used with round mallets of different sizes, the most desirable of which had lignum-vitae heads for extra weight and durability. There is a superb set of carving and cabinet makers' tools which belonged to Thomas Seaton in 1796 in the Guildhall Museum, Rochester. All the cutting tools had to be kept very sharp, and a large grindstone, sharpening stones and honing strops were all essential equipment. One of an apprentice's first tasks was to learn how to sharpen his tools. Later workshops might also have some powered machinery. When Thomas Anderson's business at Bristol was closed in 1936, the auction included a circular saw, facing, moulding and drilling machines powered from a dynamo turned by a gas engine.

Once the carving had been completed, the piece had to be painted. No one seems to have carried out any research into the paint work of ship carvings. Paint did not come ready-made in tins until the twentieth century, so before this pigments had to be ground by hand and then mixed with a combination of white lead, linseed oil and turpentine. There would have been a priming coat made from a mixture of white lead, some dryers and a little red lead to harden it. A common recipe for a dryer was a mixture of litharge (lead monoxide) and linseed oil boiled together. Before this primer was thinly applied, all the knots in the wood had to be treated with 'knotting' to prevent the turpentine in the knots from oozing out. The second undercoat of paint would have plenty of oil in it and added colour. This would have been followed by a third and a fourth coat which had an increasing amount of varnish to make the paint glossy. There would have been a final coast of varnish as added protection. All this painting would have been carried out in the carver's workshop. It was essential to paint in a dust-free atmosphere, and one way to achieve this was to hang wetted canvas sheets round the finished piece to prevent the wet paint from being spoiled by the dust of the workshop. Many nineteenth-century figureheads were just painted white with gilding on edgings such as lapels and pocket flaps, which saved both time and money. Once the painting had been finished, the carvings would be ready for dispatch to the shipbuilders. One of the partners of the firm would go and supervise the shipwrights who would use a block and tackle to lift it into position. Stagings were rigged below and on either side of the bow. You can see the end of one of these stagings on the left side of the photograph of the *Carib Prince*'s figurehead. The figurehead was bedded in with plenty of red lead and bolted down, and then the trailboards would be fitted.

Ship carvers did not fit the romantic image of 'the artist'. Indeed, none of the known British ones, apart

David Hughes' letterhead. (The Thomas Family)

from James Brooker of Maryport (c.1816–60), seemed to have signed their work. They did not have a rarefied existence, and they were subject to the harsh reality of making a living from their skills. In the shipbuilding industry, ship carving was one of the outfitting trades along with block making, sail making, painting and upholstery. These types of work tended to be sub-contracted rather than being part of the main shipbuilding trades. Smaller shipyards, which worked mainly on repairs and only built new

vessels occasionally, might use one of their own shipwrights to tackle the odd carving job. Certainly some of the figureheads from coasting brigs and schooners have the look of being carved by someone who had not been trained and who had only an elementary knowledge of anatomy. In *From Tree to Sea*, Ted Frost recalled his time as an apprentice in the early 1900s at a small shipyard at Lowestoft, Suffolk. It specialised in building wooden steam drifters. He remembered: 'With the hawse pipe fitted, it was now

Utah State Chair

One of David Hughes' highly ornamental pieces of furniture, the State Chair of Utah. (The Thomas Family)

possible to set out and carve the name and the scroll . . . Mr George Knights, the foreman joiner in No.3 yard, generally used to do this job for'ad while William 'Chuddy' Tills would carve the name and port of registry aft . . . Although Mr Knights had carving tools he would use an ordinary gouge for the job as the section of the name and the scroll was a simple half round.'

The late P N Thomas in his *British Figurehead and Ship Carvers* identified about 150 ship-carving firms at work in the eighteenth and nineteenth centuries. They were not all working at the same time and some are only known from one reference. He was also able to identify many of the Master Carvers who worked in the naval dockyards. The majority of firms working on merchant ship figureheads were based in the main centres of shipbuilding, the heaviest concentrations being on the Clyde estuary from Greenock to Glasgow and in the North East of England split between the Rivers Tyne, Wear and Tees. Other shipbuilding ports with more than one firm of ship carvers were Aberdeen, Dundee, Liverpool, London and the Cumbrian ports of Whitehaven, Workington and Maryport. All the other major ports such as Bristol had at least one ship-carving business. I am not aware of any equivalent studies for other countries, but the same principle certainly applied – ship carvers had to be close to their customers.

None of these businesses were especially stable,

although there were exceptions like the Hellyer family who were main contractors to the naval dockyards with a continuing succession of contracts. Shipbuilding was a notoriously cyclical business where a boom in orders was followed by a complete drought because too many ships had been built. For example, in the early 1850s, there was a huge demand for ships stimulated by the discovery of gold in California and Australia. Both distant places needed large ships to transport huge numbers of gold diggers and vast quantities of supplies to sustain them. Furthermore, the outbreak of the Crimean War stoked up demand further because large numbers of ships were needed to transport troops, horses, ordnance and all their other supplies. But by 1857, both the war and the Gold Rushes were over and as a result there was glut of new ships seeking work and shipbuilders were left struggling to fill their order books. The risk of insolvency haunted all small firms in the nineteenth century. Most were run by families or partners with unlimited liability, and the bankruptcy of a shipyard and its failure to pay could put a ship carver out of business as well. Many sought to spread their risks by undertaking several different types of carving. The Glasgow firm of Kay and Reid was established in 1857 after the break-up of an earlier partnership when James Reid joined forces with the widow of Thomas Kay, who had died in 1852. Under his leadership the firm expanded from five apprentices and five journeymen in 1861 to a staff of over thirty by 1871. One of their advertisements demonstrated their range of work: ship, architectural and cabinet carvers, pattern makers, gilders, decorators, picture frame makers, print sellers, dealers in works of art, oil painting restorers and suppliers of artist's materials. Some of their financial details have survived in the ledgers of Clyde shipbuilders. For example, in 1879 interior 'egg and dart' (a standard

Classical pattern) cornice moulding was priced at 2s 2d per foot and large capitals were 7s each. These were part of an order from Connells for the fitting-out of the cargo liner *City of Agra*. A figurehead, trailboards, stern carvings and 'finishes on the poop' for a sailing ship being built by Russell & Co. in 1867 cost £13 10s, with another £13 18s 8d spent on carvings for the main saloon and cabins. In 1865, the Union Shipbuilding Co. went bankrupt owing them £68 16s 6d. Bearing in mind the sample prices I have just quoted, that debt represented a large amount of work for the firm. At least one ship-carving firm built up stocks of carvings for immediate delivery, meaning they could provide themselves with work in slack times and make quick deliveries provided the shipbuilder's customer did not want a particular figurehead. In 1843 Archibald and John Harriott of North Shields advertised that they had 'constantly on hand' a great variety of male and female busts, drops, stars, lion's faces, together with a large quantity of ship's ornaments, for acute and obtuse angles. The drops and the stars were for decorating the stern and the lion's faces were for the catheads.

Carvers often moved to find work. Thomas Johnson, who wrote his autobiography, was apprenticed in London. He came out of his indentures in 1744 and by 1747, he had moved to Liverpool. After a year there, he moved to Dublin for eight months and then returned to Liverpool to set up his own workshop with twelve journeymen. They worked not just on figureheads, but also on carvings for houses, St George's Church and the Liverpool Exchange. By 1753 he was back in Dublin and sometime early in 1755, he was offered work back in London. This in turn led to the opportunity to publish his ornamental designs, which brought him financial success. However, by 1764 he was made bankrupt. From then until his death in 1799, he seems to have lived on a combination of jobs including acting as clerk to the Charlotte Street Chapel, Bloomsbury, carving and writing.

David Hughes was an example from the time when the demand for ship carving was declining rapidly. He was born the son of a Liverpool cotton porter in 1847. By 1861 he was working his apprenticeship as a cabinet maker. He married in 1868 and his marriage certificate gave his job as ship carver. His frequent changes of residence – on average once a year – suggested that his finances were not in a good state. In 1890, he was able to set up his own business in a workshop in Chaloner Street, close to the South Docks. It consisted of a ground floor showroom, a first floor workshop and a flat on the top floor. His letterhead describes the firm which included two of his sons as 'ship, figure, cabinet and architectural carvers. Reproductions of antique furniture a speciality. Lessons given in wood carving.' His photographs that have been passed down to his descendants show that he did win new commissions for figureheads. It was not a propitious time because the four shipyards on the Liverpool side of the Mersey had closed down by 1894. They had tended to specialise in sailing ships as well. Lairds, the only other local yard located at Birkenhead, built almost nothing but steamers, although they did build the steam and sail training ship *Presidente Sarmiento* for the Argentine Navy in 1899, and it is possible that Hughes carved her figurehead and trailboards. She was last ship to be built with a clipper bow on the Mersey. He therefore developed the furniture side of the business. In 1897, one piece, an elaborately carved settle summarizing the achievements of Queen Victoria's reign, received favourable comment in *The Architect* and the *Shipping Telegraph*, but it does not seem to have brought in a rush of commissions. It is likely that he carved the dwarf figures that support the first floor of the mock Tudor frontage of Rigby's Hotel in Dale Street, Liverpool. There is also another similar piece – a man seated on a tub in a stocking cap and sea boots with a mirror embedded in his stomach – in private hands. In 1907, he emigrated to Utah and ended up teaching carving at the local state college – a long way from the sea and figureheads. At least he did not suffer the fate of poor James Brooker, who had received great acclaim for his work including winning a medal for one his figureheads at the Great Exhibition in 1851. In 1853, he moved from Maryport to Glasgow to seek work. Within a year, he had moved on to Sunderland and by 1859 he was back in Maryport. The following year he was admitted to the local workhouse as a pauper where he died within months.

The ship carver's training was by an apprenticeship which usually lasted seven years. At first he would be given simple pieces to carve such as a rope moulding. Once out of his indentures, he became a journeyman who was free to seek employment wherever he wished. As with other working men, ship carvers were paid by the day. There were exceptions, however. Pierre Puget (1620–84) began work as an apprentice carving decoration for the French navy's galleys at Toulon. His exceptional talent was recognised and he was sent to the studio of Pietro da Cortona, the leading Italian sculptor of the Baroque era. On his return to France, he not only undertook ship carving but worked on major artistic projects for King Louis XIV including his new palace at Versailles. In the eighteenth century French carvers were believed to be at the summit of artistic achievement and the leading naval ship carvers of other continental navies were influenced or had trained in France. This included a succession of chief carvers for the Danish Navy and Johan Törnström of Sweden. Törnström (1743–1828) had been a pupil of J B Maserliez, a Frenchman working

at Stockholm. He worked on carvings for ships and the Royal Palace in the Swedish capital until 1781. In that year Chapman, the chief naval architect to the Swedish Navy, persuaded him to come and work exclusively on ships' carvings at the Karlskrona naval base. His large Neo-classical figures, some of which were over ten feet high, were carved from oak and could take up to two years to finish. When the Swedish Navy suspended building new ships in 1790, he found himself having to diversify into carving for churches to support his family of ten children. So, even one of the greatest of all ship carvers was not protected from economic forces and the same applied to all artists and craftsmen until the late twentieth century. Ship carving was a precarious calling and one that required its practitioners had the versatility to be able to turn to other kinds of work.

An odd piece of furniture by David Hughes. (Private Collection)

Figurehead Survivors

In most cases the figureheads and ship carvings which survive have out-lived the ships for which they were carved. They have been saved for a variety of reasons: their decorative qualities, as curios, for their monetary value, very occasionally as trophies of war or as memorials to drowned sailors. Occasionally, they survive with their ship. By far the largest number are from nineteenth-century sailing ships belonging to European or North American owners. As they voyaged to every part of the world and were wrecked or scrapped well away from their home ports, they can be found in some very remote places. The sheer number of sailing ships wrecked was staggering. For example, according to the Board of Trade statistics, between 1859 and 1864 there was an annual average of 1664 shipwrecks around the British Isles. In the winter gales, hundreds might be cast ashore in a single night. The Great Gale of 26 October 1859 saw 344 casualties, including the auxiliary sailing ship *Royal Charter* which went ashore on Anglesey with the loss of over 400 passengers and crew. These awful statistics gradually decreased in the second half of the nineteenth century, partly because of the increasing use of steamers, and partly because of a combination of better regulation, navigational aids and rescue services. The sailing ship without an engine was particularly vulnerable when making a landfall. Cloud cover or fog could prevent the ship's officers from getting an accurate position from the sun or the stars, and it was then fatally easy for the master to make an error and put his ship on to the rocks or sandbanks. Onshore

The headquarters of the Old Company at Lowestoft about 1900.

Headquarters of the Old Company of Lowestoft Beachmen circa 1900.

The headquarters of the Sunderland Volunteer Lifesaving Association. (A J Lewery)

winds could also drive a ship to destruction. The old tales of 'wreckers' deliberately luring ships on to rocks with false lights are almost certainly myths, but even so, there were plenty of people on the coast who made a living from assisting vessels in distress. There were salvage companies or boatmen at places of hazard where large numbers of ships passed, which included the Scillies, Deal on the Kent coast opposite the Goodwin Sands, and the East Anglian coast from Southwold to Sea Palling. The boatmen could go out to a ship to help with pilotage or pumping or salvaging cargo. A figurehead might not be a priority salvage item, but some ended up as

trophies in their headquarters. The front gable of the Lowestoft Old Company's shed was decorated with two figureheads, carved nameboards and stern badges in the 1930s, and the headquarters of the Sunderland Volunteer Lifesaving Association is still a treasure-house of ship carvings.

Shipbreaking became an established industry in the nineteenth century, and the most important shipbreaking yards were on the Thames. They specialised in taking apart high quality ships such as warships or East Indiamen whose large timbers could be sold on for re-use in buildings and the construction of new ships. Their copper sheathing

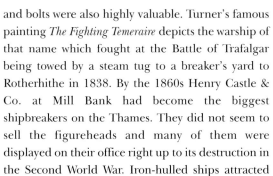

Left: Stern carvings on the Admiral's Office, Chatham. (Chatham Historic Dockyard Trust)

Far left: The restored figurehead of the *Vera Jean.* (National Museums Liverpool)

and bolts were also highly valuable. Turner's famous painting *The Fighting Temeraire* depicts the warship of that name which fought at the Battle of Trafalgar being towed by a steam tug to a breaker's yard to Rotherhithe in 1838. By the 1860s Henry Castle & Co. at Mill Bank had become the biggest shipbreakers on the Thames. They did not seem to sell the figureheads and many of them were displayed on their office right up to its destruction in the Second World War. Iron-hulled ships attracted

other firms who had links with firms who needed scrap metal. Firms such as T W Ward of Sheffield established yards at places with access to steel works such as Newport, Monmouth and Preston. They dismantled large numbers of sailing ships and steamers with figureheads and interior carvings. Most of the interior carved work was readily sold to furnish hotels or public houses. By the early twentieth century the figureheads were also sold because by then there was a growing interest in

Right: Female bust, possibly from a sailing coaster, at Southwold.

Far right: Standing figure at Southwold. The bunch of grapes suggests that she was from a fruit schooner.

sailing ships. In the 1920s Wards broke up the three-masted iron ship *Vera Jean* at Preston, and her figurehead was bought by a Preston architect, the late Sir Grenfell Baines, who eventually used it as a decoration on the wall of Lancashire Fire Brigade's training school at Euxton miles from the sea.

There are also ships or boats that have somehow survived intact with their carvings. They might be still working as sailing training vessels. Many of the naval ones such as the Spanish Navy's *Juan Sebastian De Elcano* built in 1928 are now old vessels. There are also much older craft that have been preserved

under cover, mainly royal barges. The *Kadirga*, the Turkish sultan's gallery which is in the Naval Museum at Istanbul, certainly dates back to the seventeenth century, and there is a theory that she might be older and date back to 1453. Another less well-known royal barge is the felucca belonging to King Charles III of the Two Sicilies (1716–88) preserved at the San Martino Museum at Naples. At the bow, this has an upright sea-lion (a lion with a fish's tail), holding a crown in its fore paws and beakhead projecting beyond it which is finished off with a dragon. The pavilion at the stern has

Right: A possible naval figurehead that advertises a ship chandler's shop at Falmouth.

Far right: The warrior of the Tantons Hotel, Bideford.

elaborate carvings in relief and the there is a large coat of arms on the stern itself supported by two life-sized figures. This is similar in splendour to the state barges owned by the National Maritime Museum, used by the Royal Family as water transport on the Thames. The finest of these is the barge belonging to George II's heir Frederick, the Prince of Wales of 1732, designed by the leading architect of the time,

A second figurehead over the entrance to the shop chandlery has been posed as if she were on a ship.

William Kent and carved by John Richards who had succeeded the famous Grinling Gibbons as Master Carver to the Crown. All of these lovely vessels can give you a feeling of the exuberance of the carvings that adorned ships in the seventeenth and eighteenth centuries.

Navies have been great preservers of figureheads. They can be found in dockyards and naval bases. Naval training schools were frequently started in old wooden warships and transferred ashore, and when that happened the figurehead went too and was set up in a free standing position or cantilevered out from the side of a building. Some navies took more care than others. Those belonging to the Swedish Navy at the Karlskrona naval base have survived intact because they have been kept under cover, but many in the British dockyards were set up outside and then not maintained. The result has been the loss of many fine pieces. An Admiralty census of figureheads

carried out in 1911 revealed that there were approximately fifty-three at Chatham, fourteen at Sheerness, fifteen at Portsmouth and seventy-two at Devonport, but only a fraction of these have survived to the present day. For example, the original figurehead of HMS *Warrior* of 1859 was displayed at Sheerness and was allowed to rot away. Others have suffered rot and have been taken indoors and fibre-glass resin replicas made to stand outside. Other carvings have been incorporated into buildings. The Admiral's Office of 1808 at Chatham has the pair of mermaid stern quarter carvings and a taffrail carving at its main entrance.

Figureheads were also preserved in other places than dockyards and salvage companies. Local landowners whose estates bordered the coast might claim them from a wreck. The third Baron Newborough, Spencer Wynn had a seaside residence at Fort Belan on the Menai Straits. He was the witness to several wrecks and salvaged the

Eighteenth century stern-quarter carving used as a lintel on a barn at Crantock, Cornwall. (Captain G Hogg)

At Appledore, a house entrance with a distinctly nautical feel to the carvings.

figurehead of the *William Turner* and the stern carving from the *Jane* in the 1840s. Fortunately, he had them stored in one of his boathouses where they remained until 1987. Augustus Smith built up a remarkable collection on the island of Tresco, one of the Scilly Isles. Smith leased the islands in 1834 and began to develop their economy as a benevolent landlord. In 1841, he acquired the figurehead of the steamer *Thames*, which had been smashed on the treacherous rocks of the islands with the loss of everyone on board. From then until his death in 1872, he regularly acquired new figureheads from local wrecks, and he built a special pavilion in his garden to protect them. His successors expanded the collection and there are twenty-eight full-size pieces besides carved fragments.

Saving and displaying figureheads was not just an aristocratic hobby. Figureheads can be found on ordinary houses, pubs or shops in some coastal towns. Their numbers have gradually reduced over the years as they have either rotted away or been taken down for display indoors, but Southwold in Suffolk still has a few left as well as others displayed in the Sailor's Reading Room and the local museum. All of them were from small coastal brigs or schooners which passed the town in their thousands in the nineteenth century. Bideford, a coastal port which owned some of the last working schooners, has a fine standing Classical warrior in a niche over the entrance to Tantons Hotel. His dramatic pose suggests that his carver was influenced by Törnström. The niche in which he is set has undoubtedly helped to protect him from the worst of the weather. As with so many surviving figureheads, his origins have been lost. A ship chandler's shop on the waterfront at Falmouth has a large bust of a lady

Appledore again, a Baroque piece that looks as if it came from an entry port of a warship.

The figurehead of the brig *Caledonia* marking the grave of her drowned crew at Morwenstow. (J & C McCutcheon)

who looks as if she may be from a nineteenth-century frigate. She bears similarities to the figurehead of HMS *Diana* carved by George Williams at Chatham, particularly in the style of the mouth, hair, eyes and neckline. The building has a second figurehead which has been mounted over the entrance with the walls on either side painted to look the sides of a ship. A barn at Cranstock in Cornwall has a part of an eighteenth-century stern quarter carving as a lintel, but it was obviously considered just a useful size of timber rather being erected for decoration. The streets of the Devonshire port of Appledore have another delight. The porches of many of its houses and shops in its narrow streets are decorated with brackets like billet heads and other carvings such as lions' masks and eagles. No one knows who

carved them, but they all have a distinctly nautical look to them. Figureheads were sometimes set up as memorials to lost ships and their crews. The churchyard at Morwenstow, Cornwall still has the figurehead of the *Caledonia*, which was wrecked on the nearby coast in 1842 and most of her crew were drowned. The local vicar, the Reverend Hawker, helped to rescue the survivors and set up the figurehead on the grave of the *Caledonia*'s crew. There were certainly other figureheads set up in churchyards and on clifftops overlooking the sites of wrecks along the north Cornish coast.

There are plenty of indoor survivors. They are occasionally for sale in antique shops, often in unrestored condition. The large lady I spotted in a

Barnstaple shop recently is a good example. Her laurel wreath, fixed expression and tubular neck suggest that she may have come from an early nineteenth-century warship. The major auction houses such as Sotheby's, Christie's and Bonham's organise sales of maritime objects about twice a year and almost every catalogue contains a figurehead. The best individual collection was that assembled by the late Sidney Cumbers. He was born in 1875 in London, the son of a successful manufacturer of printing inks. Although he followed his father into the business and became its managing director, he had a burning enthusiasm for all things maritime from an early age. In 1932, he moved his growing collection to a house on the Thames at Gravesend, which had a fully-equipped bridge and a forecastle adorned with figureheads, ship models and other nautical relics. He presided over this treasure house in the persona of Long John Silver, his swashbuckling image reinforced by the eye patch he wore to conceal the loss of his right eye. The collection totaled 101 figureheads and carvings. When it was time to leave the 'Look

Right: The unrestored figurehead of the schooner *Rosebud*. (National Museums Liverpool)

Far right: The splendid Turkish figure on show in the shop of the Shipwreck Heritage Centre, Hastings. (The Nautical Museums Trust Ltd)

Out' in 1953, Cumbers generously donated his collection to the newly-formed Cutty Sark Trust for display on the freshly-restored clipper at Greenwich. Many of the figureheads have been restored and are displayed in her hold for everyone's delight. The Trust has carried out further research into their collection recently and as a result has been able to identify some of the unidentified figureheads. They are also undertaking a conservation programme to ensure that this, the finest collection of merchant ship figureheads, is safe for the future.

The problem with most figureheads is that their original identity is unknown. As a result all sorts of stories have grown up about them which are usually quite untrue. For example, the Red Lion at Martlesham is locally believed to be a relic of the Battle of Sole Bay between the English and the Dutch in 1672 when the British flagship *Royal Prince* blew up, but the style of the carving means that it must date from the early eighteenth century. But I do not suppose we can persuade the locals! The story about the *Vera Jean* also contains a lot of imagination. When the then unnamed figurehead was given to Merseyside County Museums in 1976, the Lancashire Fire Brigade officers told us the story

Far left: A new figurehead carved in 1992. (The North Devon Maritime Museum)

Left: The figurehead of HMS *Ganges* at Holbrook.

Mobile figureheads at the Portsmouth International Festival of the Sea 1998.

of how the training school had been converted into a base for the United States Air Force during the Second World War. They thought that she might have been taken as a souvenir from Liverpool by US airmen on a night out. All very persuasive, but in fact the real story emerged only twenty years later when Sir Grenfell Baines contacted the Merseyside Maritime Museum.

When the *Vera Jean* arrived at the Museum, she was suffering the way that many figureheads displayed in the open have suffered. She had been displayed as if she was still mounted on the bow of ship and the whole of her back exposed to the elements. A combination of drying, splitting and

An all-over paint scheme on the theatre ship *Fitzcarraldo*.

shrinking of the wood allowed rainwater to penetrate right inside and rot took hold. Fresh water can do far more damage than seawater which with its salts has preservative qualities. Also while at sea, a figurehead was in a fairly constant level of humidity whereas on land, the variations could be much greater, which encourages shrinking and cracking. There can also be a problem with displaying figureheads inside because the atmosphere can be too dry, and this will also cause splits. When the *Vera Jean* was moved to the conservation studio, it was found that her insides were a pulpy mass of wet wood fibre which could scooped out by hand. The layers of paint on her front were virtually all that was holding her together. All this rot had to be removed and replaced with a strengthening resin, and then the

many successive layers of paint had to be removed to reveal the original scheme of blue and red. The figurehead from the schooner *Rosebud* which was hung on the wall of a builder's yard at Crosby near Liverpool for over seventy years is an example of deterioration. Although she has been painted many times to protect her, she has a large split up her centre and numerous other cracks. The figurehead of HMS *Ganges* (see page 110), which was a naval training ship moored near Harwich, has ended up outside a boarding school at Holbrook near Ipswich. Although at first glance this Indian prince looks in good condition, patches of rot have started where the paint has peeled off on the back and around the neck and shoulders. He needs attention soon if he is to be saved.

Many figureheads (possibly the majority) have ended up in museums. The best collections are in naval establishments. The national maritime museums of nations such as Britain, France, Denmark, Sweden and Italy all have splendid pieces of some antiquity together with fine contemporary models. Apart from figureheads, they possess other types of ship carving such as the stern carving of the French galley *Grande Reale* of 1690 or the stern of the Swedish royal yacht *Amphion* of 1778. Merchant ship carvings are more scattered and apart from the large national maritime museums and large independent collections such as that of the *Cutty Sark*, most ports will have a specialist maritime museum or at least a gallery on local history. It is always worth looking in at the latter kind of museum because figureheads can turn up in some surprising places. At Hastings, for example, the local history museum has three fine examples and there is another down at the beach at the Shipwreck Centre. There is no up-to-date survey of museum collections of figureheads, but many museums publish information about their collections on their websites.

The carving of ship decorations has never stopped. There are still a few craftsmen who make much of their living from carving figureheads, and there is a large number of hobby woodcarvers who tackle nautical decorations as well. Many of these new figureheads never end up on ships but serve as internal decoration. A fine portrait bust of Emma Hamilton, Nelson's companion, by Norman Gashes was recently auctioned by Bonhams, and the North Devon Maritime Museum was presented with a figurehead of a nineteenth century carrying a shield bearing the museum's name by a local craft teacher, John Butler in 1993. The late Jack Whitehead was the best-known of the modern carvers. He restored many of the figureheads on the *Cutty Sark* and carved new ones for preserved ships. His biggest commission was the figurehead of the iron frigate HMS *Warrior* of 1859. Even if you cannot afford an original or a new hand carved figurehead, there are many replicas available usually cast in glass resin. For example, www.nauticalsupplyshop.com will sell you a mermaid cast in resin for $169 or in the United Kingdom you can find miniatures of figureheads in the National Maritime Museum for as little as £5. Figureheads have even inspired art students. At the Portsmouth International Festival of the Sea in 1998, local students built papier-mâché copies of some of the big figureheads in the Royal Naval Museum, which were paraded around the festival. So the interest in figureheads and ship carving continues.

The figurehead of the ocean-going paddle steamer *Demerara*, wrecked in the River Avon in 1851, was mounted on an auction house in New Quay Street, Bristol. It vanished when the building was demolished in 1937. (Bristol Industrial Museum)

Major Figurehead and Ship Carving Collections

Many museums (maritime or otherwise) have perhaps a few examples of figureheads or carvings. The larger collections tend to be in the larger maritime museums in Europe and the United States. Most of the museums tend not to have all of their collections on display at the same time, but reserve collections behind the scenes can usually be visited by appointment. Many museums also have websites which list the main items in their collections.

Denmark
Bangsbom Museum, Frederikshavn
National Maritime Museum, Elsinore
Royal Naval Museum, Copenhagen

Finland
Åland Islands Maritime Museum, Mariehamn

France
National Maritime Museum, Paris

Germany
Altona Museum, Hamburg

Italy
Naval Museum, La Spezia

Netherlands
National Maritime Museum, Amsterdam
Prins Hendrik Museum, Rotterdam

Norway
Bergen Maritime Museum
National Maritime Museum, Oslo

Portugal
National Maritime Museum, Lisbon

Spain
Barcelona Maritime Museum

Sweden
Naval Museum, Karlskrona
National Maritime Museum and the *Vasa*, Stockholm

United Kingdom
Chatham Historic Dockyard
The *Cutty Sark*, Greenwich, London
Merseyside Maritime Museum, Liverpool
National Maritime Museum, Greenwich, London
Royal Naval Museum, Portsmouth
Town Docks Museum, Hull
Valhalla Museum, Tresco, Scilly Islands

United States of America
Mariners' Museum, Newport News, Virginia
Mystic seaport Museum, Mystic, Connecticut
Peabody Museum, Salem, Maine
San Francisco Maritime Museum, California
US Naval Academy, Annapolis, Maryland

Far left: Some of the fine figureheads at Mystic Seaport Museum (Mystic Seaport Museum).

Left: President Abraham Lincoln on board the *Cutty Sark* (Cutty Sark Trust).

Bibliography

Anon., 'Les chaloupes crevettieres de la Baie de Seine', *Chasse Maree* Volume 80, pp34–47.

Anon., *Musée de la Marine Palais de Chaillot Paris* (Paris 2000).

Bailey, S F, *Cutty Sark Figureheads. The Long John Silver Collection* (Abingdon 1992). A picture catalogue of the main figureheads on the *Cutty Sark*.

Baker, W A, *The Mayflower and Other Colonial Vessels* (London 1983). An account of building of the replica of the Pilgrim Fathers' ship and a detailed account of the characteristics of early seventeenth-century merchant ships.

Basch, L, 'The *Kadirga* Revisited', *The Mariner's Mirror* Volume 65 (1979), pp39–51. A survey of this Turkish galley and new theory on the date of her building.

Bowen, F C, 'Ships' Figureheads' in *Shipping Wonders of the World* (London 1937), pp776–80.

_____, 'The *Sovereign of the Seas*' in *Shipping Wonders of World* (London 1937), pp115–17.

Brewington, M V, *Ship Carvers of North America* (New York 1962).

Briot, C and J, *Les Clippers Français* (Douarnenez 1993).

Brouwer, N J, *The International Register of Historic Ships* (3rd edition, London, 1999).

Chapelle, H, *The History of American Sailing Ships* (New York 1935).

_____, *The History of the American Sailing Navy* (New York 1949).

Cooper, J C, *An Illustrated Encyclopaedia of Traditional Symbols* (reprinted London 1999).

Corlett, E, *The Iron Ship* (Bradford-on-Avon 1983). The story of the *Great Britain*

Costa, G, *Figureheads* (Lymington 1981).

Cunliffe, T (ed), *Pilots The World of Pilotage under Sail and Oar* (Douarnenez and London 2001).

De Zulueta, J, 'The Basque Whalers. The Source of their Success', *The Mariner's Mirror* Volume 86 (2000), pp261–71.

De Cervin Abrizzi, G B R, 'An Eighteenth Century Felucca', *The Mariner's Mirror* Volume 66 (1980), pp187–98. A detailed account with plans of the state galley preserved at the Museo di San Martino, Naples.

Falconer, W, *An Universal Dictionary of the Marine* (London 1780, reprinted Newton Abbot 1970).

Farr, G (ed), 'Bristol Ships', *Bristol Record Society* Volume 15 (n.d.).

Fox, F, 'The English Naval Shipbuilding Programme of 1664', *The Mariner's Mirror* Volume 78 (1992), pp277–92. Useful pictures and descriptions of some of the lesser line of battleships built by Charles II.

_____, 'Hired Men-of-War 1664-7, part II', *The Mariner's Mirror* Volume 84 (1998), pp152–73. Includes Van de Velde drawing of *Loyal George*.

Frere-Cook, G, *The Decorative Arts of the Mariner* (London 1966).

Gardiner, R (ed), *Cogs, Caravels and Galleons: The Sailing Ship 1000-1650* (London 1994).

_____, *The Heyday of Sail: The Merchant Sailing Ship 1650-1830* (London 1995).

_____, *The Line of Battle: The Sailing Warship 1650-1840* (London 1992).

_____, *The Advent of Steam: The Merchant Steamship before 1900* (London 1993). These 'Conway's History of the Ship' volumes are up-to-date, well-illustrated and scholarly.

Greenhill, B, with Morrison, J, *The Archaeology of Boats and Ships: An Introduction* (London 1995).

Hamilton, G W, *Silent Pilots: The Figureheads of Mystic Seaport Museum* (Mystic 1984). A well-illustrated catalogue of an excellent collection.

Hanna, J S, *Marine Carving Handbook* (Camden, Maine 1972). A how-to book on carving name and stern boards in the American style.

Hansen, H J, *Galionsfiguren* (Bremerhafen 1984). A detailed list of all known figureheads in museums and public places. Most pieces are illustrated. It is in German and has an irritating code system for captioning the pictures, but there is nothing else as comprehensive as this.

Harland, John, *Ships and Seamanship: The Maritime Prints of J J Baugean* (London 2000). First published in Paris in 1819, Baugean is reckoned to be an accurate recorder of the many types and rigs of sailing ships at the beginning of the nineteenth century.

Harris, D G, *F H Chapman: The First Naval Architect and his Work* (London 1989).

Hornell, J, *Water Transport Origins and Early Evolution* (reprinted Newton Abbot 1970).

Hyde, Ralph, *A Prospect of Britain: The town panoramas of Samuel and Nathaniel Buck* (London 1994). The Bucks' engravings provide a detailed view of the British port in the early eighteenth century. The author has established that they got the ships right because they employed a marine painter to draw them.

Hutchinson, Gillian, *Medieval Ships and Shipping* (Leicester 1994). A wide-ranging and accessible account of the development of medieval ships.

Johnstone, P, *The Sea-craft of Prehistory* (London and Henley 1980).

June, J (engraver), *A New Book of Ornaments for the use of all are any way conversant in designing, carving, painting and drawing ships* (London 1799).

Kemp, P (ed), *The Oxford Companion to Ships and the Sea* (Oxford 1976).

Laughton, L G C, *Old Ship Figureheads and Sterns* (London 1925).

Leek, Michael E, *The Art of Nautical Illustration* (London 1994).

Lewery, A J, *Popular Art Past and Present* (Newton Abbot 1991).

_____, *Flowers Afloat. Folk Artists of the Canals* (Newton Abbot 1996)

Lyon, D, *The Sailing Navy List 1688-1860* (London 1996).

_____, and Winfield, R, *The Sail and Steam Navy List 1815-1889* (London 2004).

MacGregor, D R, *The Tea Clippers: Their History and Development 1833-1875* (3rd edition London 1983).

_____, *Merchant Sailing Ships 1815-1850* (London 1984).

_____, *Merchant Sailing Ships 1850-1875* (London 1984).

_____, *Merchant Sailing Ships 1775-1815* (2nd edition London 1985).

_____, *Fast Sailing Ships* (2nd edition London 1988).

The late David MacGregor's books on merchant sailing ships are standard works on their development in the eighteenth and nineteenth centuries.

Menzel, H, *Smakken, Kufen, Galioten Drei Vergessene Schiffstypen des 18 und 19 Jahrhunderts* (Bremerhafen and Hamburg 1997). Historical survey of the design and construction of German and Dutch coastal smacks, kofs and galliots, many of which had carved rudder heads.

Muscat, J, and Millot, N, 'The Dghaijsa of Malta', *Maritime Life and Traditions* Volume 10, pp54–71.

Neubecker, O (ed), *Heraldry Sources, Symbols and Meaning* (Maidenhead 1977). Well illustrated and good on the symbolic meanings of particular devices such as the lion.

Norton, Peter, *State Barges* (London 1972). A pamphlet crammed with excellent pictures and highlighting Prince Frederick's barge in the National Maritime Museum's collection.

_____, *Ship's Figureheads* (Newton Abbot 1976). Well-illustrated and wide-ranging, but sticking to figureheads and not the wider aspects of ship decoration.

Olsen, Carol, 'Stylistic developments of ship figureheads of the United States East Coast', *International Journal of Nautical Archaeology and Underwater Exploration* Volume 8 (1979), pp321–32

Osler, A, and Barrow, A, *Tall Ships and Two Rivers* (Newcastle 1993). An account of the sailing ships of Newcastle and Sunderland.

Paget-Tomlinson, E W, *Colours of the Cut: The Company Colours of the Inland Waterway Working Boats of Britain* (Ashbourne 2004).

Pastoureau, M, *Heraldry: Its origins and meaning* (London 1997). A useful introduction to the 'science' of heraldry which has relevance for the heraldic devices used on ships.

Peacock, John, *The Chronicle of Western Costume* (London 1991).

Quarm, R, 'A new acquisition for the National Maritime Museum', *The Mariner's Mirror* Volume 90 (2004), pp308–10. A detailed description of the coat of arms of James, Duke of York, which is believed to have been an internal ornament on a British warship of the late seventeenth century.

Rodger, N A M, *The Safeguard of the Sea. A Naval History of Britain, 660-1649* (London 1997). _____, *The Command of the Ocean. A Naval History of Britain, 1649-1815* (London 2004). The latest and most readable history of the Royal Navy with a further volume awaited.

Simon, J, 'Thomas Johnson's *Life of the Author*', *Furniture History*, Volume 39 (2003), pp1–64.

Soop, H, *The Power and the Glory. Sculptures of the Warship Vasa* (Stockholm 1988).

Stewart-Brown, R, *Liverpool Ships in the Eighteenth Century* (Liverpool and London 1932).

Topsail, Journal of the Society for Sailing Barge Research published annually for members has a regular feature on sailing barge decoration. Enquiries to the Membership Secretary, 21 Newmarket Road, Strensham, CB6 3JZ.

Thomas, P N, *British Figurehead and Ship Carvers* (Albrighton 1995).

Thornton, P, *Form and Decoration Innovation in the Decorative Arts 1470-1870* (London 1998). A wide-ranging account of the development of ornament in Europe of particular relevance to the Baroque decoration of warships in the seventeenth and eighteenth centuries.

Tibbles, A, *An Illustrated Catalogue of Marine Paintings in the Merseyside Maritime Museum* (Liverpool 1999).

Unger, Richard, 'Four Dordrecht Ships of the 16th century', *The Mariner's Mirror* Volume 61 (1975), pp109–27.

Waite, A H, *National Maritime Museum Catalogue of Ship Models Part 1, Ships of the Western Tradition to 1815* (Basildon, *c.*1975). A complete catalogue of all the Museum's Navy Board and other contemporary ship models to 1815 with small illustrations in which it is difficult to make out much detail of their carvings.

Wilson, T, *Flags at Sea* (London 1986). Useful on the types of banners flown by the Tudor navy.

Yarwood, Doreen, *The Architecture of Britain* (London 1990).

Index